"Sally Rogow has written a bo
indomitable spirit of humanity. Tl
young people who demonstrate tl
must never triumph, is both unique and remarkable. *Faces of Courage* is about young people, for young people, but it is a book with universal appeal. The Holocaust was a time of unspeakable malevolence. The heroes of Dr. Rogow's book provide a shining light for all of us to follow. Like *The Diary of Anne Frank, Faces of Courage* should become required reading in every high school in this country."

—Bernie Farber, Executive Director
Canadian Jewish Congress

"Sally Rogow's portrayal of acts of bravery carried out by young people during WWII provides a highly valuable source for inspiring, especially in younger readers, the basic lessons that should be learned from the Holocaust. It highlights moral qualities in ordinary people, which are centrally important during such times of oppression and persecution, and the ability and strength to care for other people, to show empathy for their suffering, and to act courageously against injustice, even in the face of adversity. *Faces of Courage* is a potent educational book, written with great sensitivity and literary talent. It illustrates its educational message through compelling historical cases, described in a simple and effective language, and thus recommends itself particularly to pedagogues and teachers."

—Dr. Gideon Greif
Yad Vashem
Jerusalem and Givatayim

"*Faces of Courage* demonstrates that heroes are not restricted by religion, gender, ethnicity or by physical or mental handicaps."

—Amanda L. Sherrington, Executive Director
Canadian Council of Christians and Jews

Faces of Courage

Young Heroes of World War II

by Sally M. Rogow

National Library of Canada Cataloguing in Publication Data

Rogow, Sally M., 1930-
Faces of courage : young heroes of World War II /
Sally Rogow ; editor, Jean Lawrence.

Includes bibliographical references.
ISBN 1-894694-20-1

1. Holocaust, Jewish (1939-1945)–Juvenile literature.
2. World War, 1939-1945–Jews–Rescue–Juvenile literature.
3. Righteous Gentiles in the Holocaust–Juvenile literature.
4. Jewish children in the Holocaust–Juvenile literature.
5. Teenagers–Europe–Biography–Juvenile literature.
6. Heroes–Europe–Biography–Juvenile literature.
I. Lawrence, Jean. II. Title.

D804.34.R63 2003   j940.53'183'0922   C2003-910932-1

Editing: Jean Lawrence, Arlene Prunkl, David Yanor
Proofreading: Arlene Prunkl
Book and cover design: Fiona Raven
Cover illustrations: Gordon Clover

First Printing October 2003

Granville Island
Publishing

Suite 212–1656 Duranleau
Vancouver, BC, Canada V6H 3S4
Tel 604-688-0320 Toll-free 1-877-688-0320
www.granvilleislandpublishing.com

Dedication

A tribute to
young heroes everywhere.

In loving memory
of my husband Robert
who was always my hero.

Acknowledgments

The author is grateful to her family, friends and colleagues for their support and encouragement. I want to especially thank Dr. Mark Nataupsky of the Holocaust Education Foundation for taking time from his busy schedule to write the Foreword. He established the invaluable, award-winning Holocaust Teacher Resource Center web site www.Holocaust-trc.org.

I am also grateful to Solly Kaplinski from the Yad Vashem for his thoughtful comments. Very special thanks go to my publisher, Jo Blackmore and her editorial team, Jean Lawrence, Arlene Prunkl and David Yanor for their talent, care, good advice and for their belief in the importance of telling these stories. Thank you also to Fiona Raven who designed the book and artist Gordon Clover, who did such a fine painting for the cover.

Contents

Map of Europe, 1939

Foreword

Faces of Courage is a major step forward in the evolution of Holocaust education. In order to learn lessons from the Holocaust, we have to identify in some way with the material. Teaching about the millions of people who were exterminated does not help us to understand what was happening. We cannot relate to those numbers alone. However, these stories about young people who lived through that time in history enable us to feel the terror of living under German occupation during World War II. Only when we identify with this reality can we learn from it and begin to take action.

Holocaust education was not taught when I was in middle school or in high school. That was in the 1950s, and it was "too early." Most Holocaust survivors did not want to talk about their horrific experiences. Sadly, most of the world either was not interested or did not believe what it heard. We had to learn the need for Holocaust education. We also needed to learn how to *do* Holocaust education. It is hoped that, if enough people learn the lessons of the horror of Nazi atrocities, then no people, no religion, no nationality, nor any "defined group" will endure such a tragedy in the future. Linking stories of the courageous young people who defied the Nazis will help us to continue to reveal the truth of what was the Holocaust and to change our behavior in order to prevent it from ever happening again.

Faces of Courage provides an essential link from the past horrors to future actions. Young people (and those of us who once were young) can be inspired by those individuals who took action and ultimately made a difference.

Mark Nataupsky, Ph.D.
Founder, Holocaust Education Foundation
Newport News, Virginia
www.Holocaust-trc.org

Introduction

If there is any light in the darkness of the Nazi era, it is to be found in the courage of those who dared to fight back, to rescue others, to join resistance movements or simply to survive. In every country occupied by the Nazis, there were people, young and old, who risked their lives to save others. *Faces of Courage* tells the stories of heroes—Danish, French, Jewish, German, Polish and Gypsy young people—whose actions made a difference. The book recounts the true stories of the young Germans who refused to join the Nazi youth movement and others who were victims of Nazi oppression. Stories of young people with disabilities who survived the hardships of Nazi persecution are also included. All are based on factual material and draw from documented sources.

Three of the stories relate the heroics of real people. Jacques Lusseyran was sixteen years old when he organized the student resistance group in Paris. He was blind. His story is based on his autobiography, *And There Was Light* (Parabola Books, 1998). The Huebener Group tells about the activities of three young Germans— Helmuth Huebener, Karl-Heinz Schnibbe and Rudolf Wobbe—who defied Hitler. The book *When Truth was*

Treason: German Youth Against Hitler (University of Illinois Press, 1995) provided the facts on which the story is based. Jacob, the story of a Polish boy, is based on a document obtained from the Yad Vashem—the Holocaust Memorial and Documentation Center in Israel.

The stories based on fictional characters tell of documented events taken from sources which can be found in the References. Every story offers another glimpse of life under the Nazi occupation of Europe during World War II.

It is important that these heroes are not forgotten. It has been inspiring for me to research and to tell these stories of hope, courage and fortitude.

1 Jacques Lusseyran

FRANCE

The true story of
a young blind leader
of the French Resistance

Jacques took Jean's arm as they made their way through the shale and brush of the hills bordering the Seine Valley. When they reached the top of the tallest hill, Jacques told him to look down. "You should be able to see the bend in the river from here," he said.

Jean looked down and saw the sparkling waters of the Seine flowing around a deep bend. "You amaze me," Jean said. "You can't see, but you know more about the hills than I do."

"Being blind makes you aware of things seeing people take for granted," Jacques replied. "There's more than one way of knowing the world."

Jacques paid close attention to the echoes that bounced off buildings as well as the mountains; he felt the ground beneath his feet and explored the shapes and textures of objects with his fingers. He knew when people were speaking to him from the direction of their voices and he discerned intention from the tones and rhythms of speech as well as words.

Jacques had been totally blind from the age of eight. His parents encouraged his love of adventure and independence. His mother taught him Braille so he could go to school with his friends, instead of attending the Institute for the Blind. In six weeks, Jacques mastered the Braille system and could read and write. He returned to school. He received good marks from his teachers and graduated from elementary school at the top of his class. After graduation, Jacques moved with his family to Toulouse in the south of France.

In June 1940, the German army invaded France and declared victory over the French. The French government was disbanded and France was divided into two zones. The northern part of the country was ruled by the Germans while the southern portion was governed by the Vichy government, who were French Nazi collaborators.

Jacques's father, an engineer, was ordered back to Paris in September. Jacques was fifteen years old.

When Jacques and his family returned to Paris, Nazi troops were stationed in the city. There were no taxis to take them from the train station to their apartment. They had to walk two miles to their apartment building on the *Boulevard Port-Royal*, a busy street on the outskirts of the Latin Quarter.

Jacques could sense the eerie silence that enveloped the city. There were no traffic sounds; the streets were empty. Even the Latin Quarter was quiet. He remembered the Latin Quarter as a lively place filled with the sounds of people talking and laughing in the outdoor cafés that dotted the streets. "It feels like the city is in mourning," Jacques told his parents.

The apartment house on the *Boulevard Port-Royal*

stood between a candy shop and a bakery. Jacques had two small rooms in his family's apartment on the fourth floor of the building. Jacques liked having his own space and arranged his furniture the way he wanted. He was ready to begin school. He planned to go to the *Louis Le Grand Lycée* with Jean. It was the best secondary school in Paris. To his dismay, he was ordered to take a special exam before he could be admitted. He had to show he was able to keep up with the schoolwork.

"People who are blind are always having to prove they are as good as others," he complained to his friends.

"Don't worry. You'll pass with flying colors," Jean said.

Jacques took the exam and did so well that he was admitted to the advanced class. But the *Louis Le Grand* was closed. The Germans closed all the schools in Paris and no one knew when they would reopen. Jacques spent his time with Jean and his other good friend, François. Eager to rediscover the city, Jacques and his friends roamed through the streets of Paris.

"The streets and buildings are the same, but the city is different," Jacques observed. "Everything is so quiet. I don't hear anyone talking; even the shopkeepers speak in quiet voices," Jacques told his friends. The lively sounds of the Paris he remembered had vanished. "Where are the German soldiers?" he asked.

"The Germans keep to themselves and stay around the Champs Élysées. They know the French don't like them," Jean told him.

"It's a good thing, too. The Nazi soldiers have done enough damage. Have you noticed how frightened people are? No one wants to talk about the Nazi occupation. Even my parents whisper to one another. They do not want our neighbors to hear them complain," François said. His family had managed to escape from Poland just before the German occupation.

"The French people are losing touch with one another. The newspapers are censored and we are forbidden to listen to British broadcasts," Jacques added. "Even the clocks are turned to Berlin time. The only sounds I can hear from my rooms are church bells."

"At least we can still enjoy a sweet French roll," Jean suggested, taking Jacques's arm and leading him into a bakery. They bought a bag of sweet rolls and munched on them as they walked. "Even the pastries don't taste the same," Jacques muttered.

When the *Louis Le Grand* school opened in October, Jacques took classes in history, philosophy and psychology. Jean came to his house early in the morning to walk to school with him. A crowd of boys always seemed to trail behind them. As they came close to the school, the concierge who stood at the main gate called out, "Here comes the Lusseyran parade."

Jacques ignored the extra attention and resented the cruel remarks some boys shouted at him. He felt like hiding when a boy yelled, "Hey, Lusseyran, how does a blind guy know where he is going?"

Jean reacted to the comments by moving close to Jacques. "Don't pay attention to the fools. They don't have half the sense you have," he told him. "Besides, with your wavy brown hair and big smile, they are just jealous of your good looks."

The boys in his classes were friendly enough and Jacques absorbed himself in his studies. He tried to ignore the morning announcements by the principal, who read Nazi news reports over a loudspeaker.

Jacques admired his history teacher; he had courage and was not afraid to voice his opinions. The history teacher was a short wiry man who never seemed to sit still. When he talked to the class about the war, he walked around the room and spoke in a loud, resonant voice.

"Hitler wants to rule all of Europe. One by one, Austria, France, Holland, Denmark and Norway have been defeated. Hitler's plan is to make all of Europe subservient to Germany. Did you know that eighty-five percent of the agricultural and industrial production of France is being sent to Germany?" the teacher told the class. He was talking so fast that Jacques found it hard to keep up with him.

"In one hour, the teacher tells us more about what is happening than you can read in the newspapers," Jacques told his friends. "He really makes you think."

The teacher gave Jacques a special assignment. He was to talk to the class and summarize everything he knew about the war.

"This is the first time I will be speaking to the whole class," he told Jean. He was nervous.

"If I know you, you'll be well-prepared," Jean told him.

On the day he was to give the report, Jacques brought lots of notes that he had written in Braille and put them on his desk. When his teacher asked him to speak, he hurriedly searched for the notes.

"I have your notes. I want you to speak, not read your notes," his teacher said.

Jacques took a deep breath and began to speak. At first he spoke in a low voice, but the longer he talked the stronger his voice grew.

"From what I've read I can tell that the war will be a long struggle. The United States will join Britain and the Russians have begun to fight. With two fighting fronts, there is no way that the Germans can win the war." Jacques ended his talk. He had spoken for nearly an hour.

When he finished, his teacher applauded and told him he summarized the facts very well. "Your presentation was well-researched and you had everyone's attention." No one was more surprised than Jacques that his talk had gone so well.

"The more I learn, the more disgusted I am with the French government. They are imitating the Nazis," Jacques told Jean. He was discovering just how brutal the Nazis and the fascist French government could be.

One evening, Jean burst into his room and told him in a trembling voice that his good friend Mr. Weissberg had been arrested. Mr. Weissberg was a Jewish scientist and a close friend of Jean's family. Jean went to his house every week for special lessons in biology. When Jean had arrived at Mr. Weissberg's house that afternoon, the concierge stopped him and told him that two German soldiers and a French policeman had come to the apartment early in the morning and arrested him. "He's an old man. He never hurt anyone in his life. They took him away because he's Jewish," Jean said, in a voice close to tears.

A few days later, on their way to school, they met with another friend who told them that his brother had been arrested. "The French police are holding him because my father enlisted in the Free French force in London. They took my brother to the *Santé* prison. I have to leave school and go into hiding."

"Come and see me if you need help," Jacques told him.

At dinner that night, his father told him that some Frenchmen had cut the telephone lines used by the German army near the coast. In retaliation, the Germans had executed ten Frenchmen.

"There is so much cruelty. People need to know what is happening. The French police are like Nazis. There are book burnings, arrests and horrible racial laws," Jacques told his friends.

"It is even getting dangerous to speak out in school. Some of the boys in our classes are joining Nazi youth clubs. They think the Nazis are good for France," François warned. "They'll report anyone who speaks out against the Nazis." Jacques was afraid for his history teacher.

The schools were shut down after a group of university students protested the Nazi takeover by celebrating the French victory over the Germans in World War I. They paraded in the streets, held up French victory signs and sang the French national anthem. The French police stormed into the streets to break up the parade and fired their rifles. They killed twenty students. The schools in Paris were closed for a month.

There were also food and fuel shortages in Paris. One night Jacques's room was so cold that it was almost unbearable. His fingers became so stiff that he could not read his Braille books. He put the books away and went to bed, but he could not sleep. A plan for organizing a student resistance group was taking shape in his mind.

"The French people need to know what's going on. They are burying their heads and don't realize what is happening right on the streets of Paris." Jacques told Jean and François of his idea to get a group of students together. "We'll write a bulletin and distribute it to the people of Paris."

Jean and François agreed. The three of us can't do it alone," Jean said. "We need to get some other boys to help us."

Jacques, Jean and François began to speak to other boys they trusted.

As soon as the school opened again, Jean and François spoke to the classmates they thought would want to help and arranged a meeting at Jacques's house.

Two days later, ten boys crowded into Jacques's little room and promised to help. Every boy was to try to recruit other students. More than fifty boys wanted to join them.

A meeting was arranged for the next week. They knew that such a large gathering would raise suspicion, so they arranged to meet in a large, old apartment building in the working class section of the city. They chose the building because people were always coming and going and strangers would not look out of place. Fifty-two boys came to the meeting and formed a secret organization called the "Volunteers of Liberty." Jacques and François were to be on the central committee.

"From now on there can be no turning back and no giving in to fear," Jacques told the group. "Remember, we have to keep our activities secret. Do not tell anyone about our meeting, not even your families. Gossip is dangerous. Too much talk will give us away," he warned.

It was agreed that no more than three boys would meet together at any one time. The central committee would keep everybody informed and act as a contact for the other students. The group planned to write a small bulletin they called *Les Tigres* to tell people about the brutality of Gestapo arrests, the torture of captured resistance fighters and the persecution of Jews. They also planned to recruit more students.

Jacques and François met often with other members of the central committee in the old apartment building. Jacques was put in charge of interviewing everyone who wanted to become a Volunteer.

"You are a good judge of character and the boys trust you," François told him.

Word about the Volunteers spread to students in other secondary schools and the university. Students who indicated they wanted to join were watched for several days or weeks by one of the original fifty-two members. Those who were considered trustworthy were told to "visit the blind man." Jacques interviewed the new recruits in his home.

Two short rings and one long ring of the doorbell told him that a volunteer had arrived. The rules were strict. No one was interviewed without an appointment and he did not interview anyone who came late.

Forced to rely on his instincts, Jacques knew he was not infallible and he was always on guard. "It's too easy to be trapped by an informer or a spy," he told his friends, and planned the interviews carefully. Nothing of importance was discussed in the first ten minutes.

During the interview, Jacques took his time and paid careful attention to tone of voice, words and silences. "I'm always suspicious of long explanations and well-rehearsed speeches. They cover lies and deceit. Anger is a difficult emotion to disguise." When he finished an interview, he would tell the student that someone from the Volunteers would notify him if he were accepted.

He recommended the boys he considered trustworthy to the central committee, which made the final decision about who was to be accepted as a member of the Volunteers of Liberty.

At first, only young students between seventeen and nineteen showed up, but after a few weeks, students from the university began to come. Jacques interviewed six hundred young men in less than a year. The Volunteers didn't think of themselves as a professional resistance group—only as students who wanted to liberate their country from the terror of Nazism. Jacques was surprised at how quickly the group had been organized. After only a few weeks, they'd begun to write, mimeograph and distribute the bulletin, *Les Tigres*, to homes all over Paris.

The boys in the central committee warned the Volunteers to be careful. "Our government, like the German Nazis, considers resistance to be a crime. They call resisters "gangs of terrorists" and tell people it is their duty to report us. They give money to informers. We have to be vigilant."

When they distributed the bulletins, the Volunteers worked in pairs. One boy would watch the doorways to the building while the other went from floor to floor, slipping *Les Tigres* beneath the doors of the apartments. To avoid attracting attention, the boys took off their shoes and tiptoed through the buildings.

The number of Volunteers grew steadily. "The group is growing, but few of my classmates are willing to join," Jacques noted with disappointment. Only six of the ninety boys enrolled in the advanced class at *Louis Le*

Grand were members of the group. "In every class there are two or three boys eager to report us to the police. Some teachers are ready to report us too."

Jacques and the other leaders warned the Volunteers not to talk about their activities at school. To further avoid detection, their meetings were never held in the same place twice and the routes to meeting places were carefully planned. With François or Jean by his side, Jacques went to every meeting.

He felt as if he were leading a double life. School-work occupied his daytime hours, but at 5:00 p.m., he became a resistance fighter. Evenings were busy with committee meetings, choosing articles for the bulletin and conducting interviews. On meeting nights, he did not get home until late. Jacques was surprised that he was able to keep up his grades.

He graduated from the *Louis Le Grand Lycée* with high honors. He planned to begin studying at the university in the fall. He took a special exam to qualify for the *École Normale Supérieure*, the most elite institution in the French university system. He was accepted and brought the letter of acceptance with him when he went to register for classes. When he arrived at the school he was told that he would not be allowed to attend. The Vichy government declared him to be ineligible because he was blind.

"You should fight the ruling," Jean urged him.

"The Volunteers are more important than my own ambitions. If I fight the ruling, I might attract too much attention and that would put the Volunteers in danger." Jacques decided to put his own future on hold and work full time for the Volunteers. He was eighteen years old.

In 1942, six hundred students were working for the

Volunteers of Liberty. Their work was recognized by the *Défense de la France,* the official Resistance connected with Charles de Gaulle and the Free French forces. Philippe, a leader of the main resistance group operating in France, contacted Jacques and asked to meet with him.

Jacques and Georges, a member of the Volunteers' central committee, went to a small restaurant to meet Philippe. In the back room of the restaurant, Philippe got up and greeted them warmly, shaking the boys' hands. Jacques immediately liked the tall man with the warm, friendly voice, calm manner and keen sense of humor. Philippe talked to them about the advantages of merging the Volunteers of Liberty with the *Défense de la France.*

"The *Défense de la France* has more funds. We have our own print shop, professional writers, a radio transmitter and a channel to the de Gaulle government in London. We also have an efficient way of collecting and distributing papers."

"The *Défense de la France* has everything we don't have," Jacques told Georges on the way home. The other members of the central committee agreed and voted to merge the Volunteers with the *Défense de la France.*

For the next six months, Jacques and Georges met with Philippe every day to draw up their plans.

"The main task is to make *Les Tigres* into a real newspaper with the power to impress readers and let them know there is an active French Resistance." Philippe was emphatic. "We'll print articles about the death camps, the torture of captured resistance fighters and news about the battle front. We want all French citizens to become resisters."

Jacques was excited. "We are now part of a major group," Jacques told the Volunteers. "We are no longer alone and isolated." Jacques and Georges were on the executive committee of the *Défense de la France*. The work was harder and more demanding than ever. *Les Tigres* was renamed *Défense de la France*. Thousands of copies of the two-page newspaper were printed and distributed all over France. A new system of drop-offs, mailboxes and secret methods of communication was arranged.

In February 1942, the Nazi government issued an order that all young Frenchmen over twenty-one years of age be sent to Germany to work as forced laborers. Thousands of young men went; the only exceptions were students and heads of families.

"This order is making more people aware of the real intentions of the Nazis. They want to make us their slaves," Jacques told the group. "More people are willing to join the Resistance now. The *Défense de la France* is growing. Eighty members of the original Volunteers are now professional underground operators." Jacques was proud of François, who was placed in charge of the Resistance in Brittany.

Jacques and Georges were responsible for the distribution of the newspaper in Paris. The two friends agreed that if one were arrested, the other would carry on the work.

One afternoon as Jacques and Georges went to the shop where the newspapers were printed, Georges told Jacques that he had seen a Gestapo officer walking back and forth in front of the building. They knew they were under suspicion. For the next three days, everyone who came out of the shop was followed. Philippe moved the print shop to another location.

Jacques and Georges warned the young people distributing the paper. "When you think someone is following you, go into a nearby bakery or grocery shop and leave by the back door. If you are near the subway, get on a train and get off at the next stop."

Défense volunteers took roundabout routes to meet up with the trucks that delivered the papers. The small trucks that brought the papers had signs, such as "fragile," "meteorological" or "optical" equipment pasted on the sides. The trucks dropped off the newspapers to various locations around the city. The Volunteers knew exactly when and where to pick up them up.

Jacques found the work exciting and challenging. The government of Free France had its offices in Algiers. General de Gaulle asked the resistance groups to coordinate their efforts, so Jacques and François met with leaders of the other groups. At one meeting he met the famous writer, Albert Camus, who was the editor of the Resistance newspaper, *Combat*.

Jacques remained in charge of recruitment. Philippe was looking for someone to coordinate the distribution of the paper to the industrial and mining communities in northern France. A young man named Elio came to his home without prior notification and told Jacques he was a native of Lille, an industrial city in the north.

He entered Jacques's room, grabbed his hand and shook it hard. "I want to give up my studies at the medical school and devote myself to the resistance movement," he said, and pulled his chair very close to Jacques. He seemed too sure of himself and too self-centered. He spoke in a condescending way. Alarm bells sounded in Jacques's head.

"He's pretentious and over-confident. I don't trust him," he told Philippe. "He bragged about how smart he is."

"He comes well-recommended," Philippe argued. "It's important that we get the newspapers into towns and cities in the north. Elio knows Lille very well. Besides, we can't afford to be too cautious," Philippe added.

Jacques agreed against his better judgment. Elio was accepted to the *Défense de la France* and went to Lille to establish a network for the distribution of the paper. Thousands of copies of *Défense de la France* were being distributed to every part of France. Jacques and Georges were busy with the distribution activities in Paris. Jacques forgot about Elio.

One morning in July 1943, two Gestapo officers and four armed soldiers knocked on the door of the Lusseyran apartment in the *Boulevard Port-Royal.* Heading straight to Jacques's rooms, they turned everything upside down in their search and scattered his Braille papers all over the floor. They found copies of the newspaper and arrested him. Jacques was worried that his parents would be arrested too. His parents knew about his secret activities, but they never interfered or discouraged him. Jacques was relieved when the Gestapo only arrested him. He could hear his mother crying as they pushed him out of the apartment, down the stairs and into a police car.

The Gestapo had a record of every one of Jacques's activities from the first day Elio had joined the *Défense de la France.* Jacques knew he had been right about Elio. His suspicions were confirmed when he saw several other Volunteers in the Fresnes prison. It was a mass betrayal; every one of his friends except Philippe had been arrested. Philippe had managed to escape.

Jacques was taken back and forth from Fresnes to Gestapo headquarters thirty-eight times. He was threatened with death, beaten and questioned for twelve hours at a time. He refused to give any useful information and was sent to Buchenwald, a concentration camp in Germany.

Starved and sickly, Jacques still managed to keep up his spirits and those of his friends. His knowledge of German and Italian enabled him to assist other prisoners.

*   *   *

The United States Third Army liberated Buchenwald in April 1945. Jacques was one of only thirty survivors of the two thousand people who were arrested in the sweep. He and Philippe were the only leaders of the *Défense de la France* to survive the war. The newspaper *Défense de la France* was renamed *France Soir* and became one of the most important daily newspapers in France.

After the war, Jacques returned to university and resumed his fight to be accepted to the *École Normale Supérieure*. He won and was admitted to the school. After graduation, he took a teaching position in Paris. In the 1950s Jacques Lusseyran moved to the United States and taught Literature, first at Western Reserve University in Ohio and then at the University of Hawaii. Tragically, he was killed in an automobile accident when he was only forty-seven years of age. Jacques Lusseyran was a true hero and a champion of freedom.

2 Louise

GERMANY

A Jewish girl
hides in Berlin

Louise had just gone to bed when she heard a loud knock at the door and a man's voice—"This is the Gestapo. We have come to search the house. We know you are hiding a Jew."

Louise leapt up from the bed, smoothed the sheets, grabbed her schoolbook and slipped into the closet. She huddled on the floor and covered her head with a pillow. Her heart was beating wildly; she could barely breathe. Fear surged through her body. Her room was in the back of the small flat and she could hear the footsteps coming close. With her eyes tightly shut, she prayed silently. Louise heard them come into her room.

Frau Münter stood in front of the closet door. "You have searched my house and can see for yourself that there is no one here," she said in a quiet voice.

"We are doing our duty. We were told you are hiding a Jew," Louise heard the officer say. We'll leave now, but we'll be back to search your house again. You are still under suspicion," the officer told her. Louise stayed in the closet until Frau Münter came back.

"You can come out now. They're gone," she said, and opened the closet door. "Come, let me help you." She offered Louise a hand to pull herself up. "We wanted so much to keep you safe," she said, with tears in her eyes. "You've only been with us a few weeks, but I'm afraid we'll have to find another place for you."

"Where will I go?" Louise whispered.

Frau Münter hugged her. "Don't worry. Try to get some rest now. My husband will be home soon. We'll make sure you are safe," she said. She brought Louise a glass of warm milk and held her hand. "My husband has a good friend who knows about hiding places," she told her.

Louise curled up in the bed. She could not sleep. Where would she go? How would she live? Why were Jews hated so much, she wondered.

Louise's mother was Jewish and her father was Christian. A union leader, Louise's father had spoken against the Nazis at a public meeting and had been arrested. As a prisoner, he could not protect his wife and daughter. They were treated like the other Jewish people in Berlin. Louise and her mother had to wear yellow stars on their clothing. Louise was not allowed to go to school anymore, and her friends shunned her. She was sixteen years old when they moved into an old rooming house. Her mother had taken a job at a small bakery in the neighborhood and earned enough money to buy food and pay the rent.

The rooming house was in the Jewish section of the city. Louise went to the Jewish school and made new friends. "I like this school much better than my old one," she told her mother. "The teachers care about us and our classes are interesting." Louise was learning about her religion and began to identify herself as a Jewish girl.

But by 1942, life had become harsh for Jewish people in Berlin. Jewish shops were destroyed, the school was closed and people were being arrested. Hitler bragged that he was making Germany "free of Jews." Louise's mother could no longer visit her father in prison. Herr Münter, her father's good friend, went to the prison to see him instead.

"Your father is a very brave man. He took all the blame for organizing the protest meeting and saved many people from being arrested," Herr Münter told her.

Louise and her mother were sure her father would be released and they would all be together again. Their hopes were shattered when Herr Münter told them that he had been sent to a labor camp in another part of Germany.

"I promised your father that my wife and I would do all we can to keep you and your mother safe from harm," he reassured them.

There were more arrests. Hundreds of Jewish people, young and old, were sent to concentration camps. Her grandparents, aunts and uncles on her mother's side were taken away. Herr Münter came to the rooming house looking very worried.

"I just found out that the Gestapo is going to round up the Jews who are still in Berlin. My wife and I want you and Louise to come and live with us. But you must come soon," he urged.

But there was no time to prepare. The final roundup

of the Jews in Berlin took place in February 1943. Louise was coming home from an errand when she saw Gestapo officers pushing people into a truck. As she passed by the bakery where her mother worked, a woman stopped her. "Stay away from the neighborhood. They arrested your mother this afternoon."

Recklessly, Louise pulled the yellow star off her coat and ran. She found herself on the busy street alongside the canal. Despair welled up inside her. She crossed the bridge over the canal and walked to the building where the Münters lived.

A group of Nazi youth was standing in front of the building. Louise ignored them. A woman carrying a bag of groceries stared at Louise as she opened the door. Louise was about to follow her in when she saw Frau Münter coming to the entranceway.

Louise went to greet her. Frau Münter put her finger to her lips and took her through a courtyard to another entranceway. They climbed a long flight of stairs to their apartment in a rear building. Frau Münter took her keys from her purse and opened the door of her flat.

As soon as she closed the door, Louise began to sob. "My mother was arrested."

Frau Münter put her arms around the girl. Frau Münter was a nurse who worked at a big hospital. On her way to work that morning she had seen the army trucks with gray canvas covers on the street. Armed SS men guarded the trucks filled with men, women and children. When Frau Münter saw Louise standing outside of the apartment building, she knew her mother had been arrested.

"You are safe here with us," she said, holding Louise close.

The Münters' small flat overlooked the courtyard of a large housing complex. The small parlor, two bedrooms and the crowded kitchen were warmed by a coal stove.

Frau Münter showed her to a little room with a narrow bed, a table and a chair. "This will be your room," she told her. "Stay away from the window," she warned. "We don't want the neighbors to see you."

When Herr Münter came home, his wife told him Louise was there. "If only they had come home with me sooner," he told his wife, and went to talk to Louise. He found her curled up on the bed. She turned to look at him. He could see the sorrow in her eyes.

"You did the right thing to come to us. We will look after you," he assured her. After dinner, she sat with them in the parlor. "We must take care that you are not seen by the neighbors. Most people mind their own business, but there are a few people who are suspicious of anyone new in the building. For a bag of sugar or flour, they are willing to report their suspicions to the Gestapo," he explained. He spoke to her as if she were an adult, not a young girl of sixteen.

"You must not leave the flat until I can get you a new identification card. During the day you'll have to stay in your room and not walk around. You won't be able to listen to the radio or answer the door."

Louise nodded. She knew they were endangering themselves by hiding her.

"When you have a new card you'll be able to go out." Herr Münter smiled kindly. "I know it won't be easy."

"I'll make sure no one sees me," Louise promised. She took her identification card with the big "J" on it and gave it to him. He tore the card into little bits.

Frau Münter held her hand. "When we have visitors, you'll need to stay in your room too," she said in a soft voice. "I'm really sorry things have to be this way."

"I'll be very quiet," Louise promised.

Frau Münter understood her fear and sorrow and brought her books and puzzles to keep her busy. She even managed to find schoolbooks so Louise could keep up with her studies. Each day after breakfast Louise returned to her room. She read her books, did schoolwork and worked on the puzzles. She looked forward to the evenings with the Münters. When they came home from work, Louise was able to come out of her room. She helped Frau Münter prepare dinner. Afterwards they played cards and listened to the radio. If a Nazi speech came on, Herr Münter would turn the radio off.

"I want to hear sensible talk and not propaganda," he remarked. "The sooner Hitler loses this war, the better. Then life will be good once more. Your father will be out of jail and your family will be together again," he told Louise.

When the visitors came, Louise went into her room and closed the door. As soon as the visitors left, Frau Münter would knock on the bedroom door and tell her to come out for a cookie or a chat. Louise felt safe until the Gestapo officer came.

Frau Münter discovered that it was their neighbor who had reported them to the Gestapo. The neighbor had seen Frau Münter bring Louise to the flat. When she had asked about the young girl who was living with them, Frau Münter told her that Louise was her niece who had come to visit. The woman became suspicious when she watched the flat and did not see Louise leave. She reported the Münters to the Gestapo.

When Herr Münter came home on the night of the raid, he knew that other arrangements had to be made for Louise. He knew a man who made false identification cards. The man had contact with people who were hiding Jews. Herr Münter brought Louise a new identification card and the address of a house where she would be hidden.

"You will be safer there," he told her early the next morning. "There are other young Jewish people there." He asked her to memorize the address.

"Just be careful that no one sees you enter the building. If there is someone on the street, don't go inside," he warned.

He gave Louise a wallet with some money. Frau Münter gave her a pretty new skirt and blouse that she had bought for her. Louise quickly put on her new clothes. When she was ready, Frau Münter gave her a small paper bag with a sandwich and fruit. Tearfully, the Münters hugged Louise. "You are brave like your father," Herr Münter told her.

"I'll never forget all you have done for me," Louise said quietly, and left the flat.

The waters of the canal sparkled in the early morning sunlight. Careful not to draw attention to herself, Louise kept pace with other people walking by the canal on their way to work.

The house she was looking for was on the other side of the canal. She crossed the bridge and skirted the edge of a large park. It was a part of Berlin that she had not seen before. She stopped walking when she saw the address. It was a deserted building and it looked as if no one lived there. No one else was in the street.

Louise rapped on the door four times, paused, then

rapped four more times, just as Herr Münter had instructed her. The door opened just wide enough to let her enter. Louise went inside. A tall boy stood in front of her. She recognized him at once. It was Gabriel, a boy she knew from the Jewish school. He was a musician and had often played his violin at the school. He was a year older than Louise.

"I'm glad to see you," Gabriel shook her hand.

"Did you know I was coming?" she asked.

"I didn't know it would be you, but I was told to watch for a young girl," he replied. Gabriel explained that he was a leader of a group that hid Jewish young people. "Some people call us the "U-Boats" because we are a secret group. We take care of one another and make sure that everyone has a safe place to sleep and food to eat."

Gabriel told her that she would meet some members of the group that evening. He took her to a room in the back of the building and told her the rules.

"We never do anything to draw attention to ourselves, like walk around in groups or wear funny clothing. When you see someone you know, walk away as quickly as you can. "We are going to survive this cruelty and chaos. The most important thing is to be ready to help one another."

Gabriel was confident. He was the group leader, but he never left the house during the day. He did not have a Nazi uniform. A young man who was not wearing a Nazi uniform was sure to draw suspicion. As the group leader, Gabriel kept everyone in touch with one another.

"Each person has a job to do," he explained. "Some of us buy the food; others deliver it to the hiding places.

We are very careful. There are spies on the street looking for Jewish people."

Whenever young Jews were found to be homeless, Gabriel or one of the others found places for them to live. Some of them lived in deserted buildings or cellars, while others slept behind the counters in grocery or fruit stores. The members of the group who had false identity cards were able to work. They supplied the food for those who did not have cards. Gabriel told her that some people were willing to smuggle Jews out of Berlin and help them find safe places in rural districts. A few of their members were living in small farming communities.

That night, Gabriel took her to meet the other members of the group at a small café a few blocks away. "No other city has as many cafés as Berlin," he said. "In this part of the city, there's one on almost every street." The small cafés were called *kneipen*. He took Louise into a room at the back.

After Gabriel had introduced her, the other members of the group told her about themselves. Hilde was sixteen; she worked in a laundry run by her Christian aunt. She told Louise that whenever someone in uniform came into the laundry, she had to run away. Bruno had false identification papers and worked in a factory. He delivered food to those who had no papers. He was fifteen. Anna did not have an identification card. She slept under a bed in a Christian friend's house. During the day she traveled on streetcars or went to train stations.

"At the train station, I pretend to wait for a train. When I see a soldier or a Gestapo officer, I hide in the public toilet," she explained. She was seventeen.

Louise was not the only new person in the group

that night. Leon was seventeen. He had thought he was safe until a few days before. He worked in an armaments factory in North Berlin where there were some other Jewish workers. A young Frenchman who worked with him saw him at the train station and warned him to go home, because the Gestapo would be coming to the factory to arrest Jewish workers. The next morning, the Frenchman came to his house to tell him that the Gestapo had his name and address and would be coming to get him.

"That fellow saved my life," he said. He then left his house and on the street met a boy who brought him to Gabriel.

Ilse was the daughter of a Christian mother and Jewish father. Her blonde hair and blue eyes made her look like other German girls. Her mother died when she was a small girl and she lived with her Jewish grandparents. When her grandparents and father were arrested, she went to her Christian aunt, who got her an identity card from a priest. Ilse worked as a waitress in a small restaurant. She explained that she never stayed in any place for more than a few months.

"I just don't want people to know me too well," she told the group. "You never know who's going to give you away." Ilse helped Gabriel find hiding places for new members.

After they got acquainted, Gabriel talked about remembering Jewish traditions.

"We must never forget our Jewish heritage," he said. "If we do, we are letting the Nazis win." Everyone agreed. Then Gabriel got down to business. "We know there are other young Jews on the streets who need places to hide. We need to be on the lookout for them.

And we need to keep in touch with those who cannot come to our meetings," he told them.

When the meeting was over, Ilse invited Louise to come home with her. She lived in a tiny room in an old rooming house.

"The owner is an elderly woman. She only wants the rent for the rooms and never asks people for their identity cards." Louise went home with Ilse. She had a lot in common with the blonde-haired girl. They both came from homes with one Jewish and one Christian parent. Louise had not thought of herself as being Jewish until she went to the Jewish school. Ilse's grandparents were not religious.

"I never really thought about my religion until my father and grandparents were arrested," she told Louise.

The Allies began heavy night bombing raids against Berlin in 1943. The attacks brought new dangers. People without identity cards could not use the underground air raid shelters. At the same time, the bombings made it easier to find hiding places in abandoned buildings.

There were many homeless people seeking shelter after their homes had been destroyed. Mothers with crying children, elderly people carrying luggage and other people filled the streets after the air raids. Police patrolled the air raid shelters and often asked to see identification cards.

Louise had the card Herr Münter got for her. The name "Alice Wissen" was printed on the card. Gabriel told her it was safe to use it. With her card, she was able to go to the air raid shelters with Ilse. The others had to hide in cellars and avoid injury from falling bombs and debris.

One night when Louise was in a bomb shelter, a girl she knew from her old school recognized her and called her name. Louise tried to ignore her, but when the girl persisted, Louise said, "You must have the wrong person. My name is Alice, not Louise."

The girl stared at her and shrugged. "Louise was Jewish, so I guess she's not around any more," she said casually to another girl.

Gabriel discovered a fourteen-year-old Jewish boy hiding in the cellar of a bombed-out building. He gave Louise a parcel of food and clothing to take to him. The entranceway to the derelict building was covered in rubble. Louise made her way into the cellar and found the boy sitting in a corner. He looked very frightened. Louise gave him the parcel. He tore the paper and began stuffing the food in his mouth. She had never seen anyone eat so quickly and knew the boy was starving.

Before Gabriel found him, the boy had survived by eating scraps of food from garbage cans. Quietly, she placed the clothing next to him and whispered that she or someone else would look after him. Walking through the deserted, bombed-out street with the image of the starving, skinny boy deeply etched in her mind, Louise was determined to help the group in every way she could.

With her new identity card, she traveled around the city and took parcels of food to hiding places all over Berlin. She remembered how elegant the city had been before the war. Wide boulevards and tree-lined streets were the pride of Berlin. Now the same streets were littered with rubble. Beautiful old buildings had been destroyed. The Nazis were using Berlin's most graceful synagogue as a warehouse.

The British and Americans are bombing our city, but it is Hitler who is responsible for all the grief and the damage, Louise thought to herself. She felt sorry for all Germans, not only Jews.

The young people continued to meet almost every night. They developed a strong sense of identity with one another. One of the favorite topics of conversation was what they would do when the war was over. When they heard that the Russian army was fighting Nazi troops inside Germany, hope rose like a flame and they began to talk about making plans for the future.

In the spring of 1945, the Allied armies captured Berlin. White sheets were hung from windows and on the lampposts that were still standing. Louise was reunited with her father. Her mother had been killed in a death camp. Everyone in the group survived. Gabriel and many of the others left Germany after the war and now live in Israel.

*   *   *

There were a few groups of young Jewish people who hid in Germany. They lived in empty warehouses, bombed-out buildings and rat-infested cellars. There was always the danger of being recognized and reported, and they lived in constant fear. A group called the Chug Chaluzi was organized in 1942 by Edith Wolff and saved many young people from deportation. Members of the group organized meals and lodgings for one another and met regularly in secret to exchange information. Most of the members of the group survived.

3

The Edelweiss Pirates

GERMANY

Young Germans
who defied Hitler

"I want a brutal, domineering, fearless, cruel youth. Youth must be all that. It must bear pain. There must be nothing weak and gentle about it. The free, splendid beast of prey must once again flash from its eyes. That is how I will eradicate thousands of years of human domestication. That is how I will create the New Order."

— Adolph Hitler

"Hitler's power may lay us low,
  And keep us locked in chains,
  But we will smash the chains one day,
  We'll be free again.
  We've got the fists and we can fight,
  We've got the knives and we'll get them out.
  We want freedom, don't we boys?"

(song of the Edelweiss Pirates)

Franz was late for the Nazi Youth meeting. He rushed into the room and did not salute the picture of Hitler on the wall. As he made his way to an empty seat, Herr Schmidt stopped him. "It is the rule that everyone who enters this room salutes the Führer." The big poster with Hitler's picture covered one wall of the room.

Franz ignored him and walked to an empty seat. Herr Schmidt came up to him and grabbed his shoulder. "Salute the Führer," he shouted.

"And what if I don't?" Franz said defiantly.

Herr Schmidt shook him and raised his fist.

"So now you're going to beat me," Franz said. The other boys stared at him. No one ever talked back to Herr Schmidt. He was the head teacher at the school and the leader of the Nazi Youth group.

"You are not wearing your uniform, you are late and you don't show respect to the Führer," he said in a loud voice. "You will be punished. You can't march with us tonight."

"Then march without me," Franz said. Before Herr Schmidt could stop him, he left the room. He knew he was in trouble, but he felt some satisfaction in standing up to the leader. He'd had enough of Herr Schmidt's bullying. Marching on the streets and chanting Hitler slogans was not his idea of a good time. He only went to meetings to keep his father out of trouble.

Franz lived in Düsseldorf, a big industrial city on the Rhine River in western Germany. His father worked in a steel mill and had been a leader of the steelworkers' trade union. When Hitler took over the government, the union organized protest demonstrations and many steelworkers were arrested. The Nazi government put

an end to the democratic trade union movement in
Germany.

Afraid for his family, Franz's father withdrew from
political activity, but he made no secret of his disagree-
ment with Nazi policies. He refused to let Franz join the
Jungvolk, the Nazi club for young boys. But in 1939,
Franz turned fourteen. Boys between the ages of fourteen and eighteen had to join a group of the Nazi
Youth.

"I didn't raise you to be a Nazi," his father told him.
"That's not what I want you to be." Franz did not join
until his father received a letter from the government
threatening him with loss of his job and arrest.

As soon as Franz found out about the letter, he told
his father, "I'll join the group in my school and go to
the meetings. I won't let you to jail." The next day he
joined the Nazi Youth.

At first he did not mind the meetings. He liked
sports and physical activities and paid little attention to
the speeches and slogans. But when Herr Schmidt became the club leader, everything changed. The man
was a fanatic Nazi and expected instant obedience.

"You are Hitler's boys and will do as you are told.
Youth must obey. Only those who obey can become
leaders," he told them. He put the picture of Hitler on
the wall and insisted that everyone salute it when they
entered the room. Instead of sports activities, there
was rifle practice and long marches on the main
streets of the city. Franz was bored and he felt like a
prisoner.

"We do nothing but wave flags and shout "*Heil Hitler*." Herr Schmidt tells us we must be willing to die for
the Fatherland," Franz complained to his father. "The

other boys are like sheep and do everything Herr Schmidt tells them."

His father nodded. "Nazis are brutes. Just try to keep out of trouble," he warned.

"I keep my mouth shut, but I can't promise to follow every order. I'm not a sheep and I won't act like one," Franz said, and continued going to the meetings. He showed his defiance by coming late and not wearing his uniform. He gave a quick salute to the picture on the wall only when he thought Herr Schmidt was watching him.

As he ran home through the dark streets of the working class section of Düsseldorf, Franz told himself, I'm never going to another meeting. Herr Schmidt was always shouting and giving orders. He made up his mind to leave school. He was almost sixteen—old enough to quit. Some of his friends worked in the factories and were able to avoid going to meetings. It was harder for the government to keep track of boys who worked full time than those who were still in school.

Franz raced up the stairs of the large apartment building and burst into his family's small suite. As soon as his mother saw him, she knew there was trouble.

Franz's face was flushed. "I'm quitting school. I can't go to any more meetings." Franz told his parents that he was in big trouble with Herr Schmidt. His father put his arm around him. "It had to come to this," he said quietly. "You are old enough to leave school. The steel mill needs workers now. So many men are going into the army. I'll get you a job at the mill."

Franz's father got him a job as an unskilled worker in a steel mill. He met Berthold at the steel mill. The tall friendly boy showed Franz around the mill and explained the work he would be doing. Franz liked him right away. He was a year older than Franz, but he took an interest in him. Berthold made no secret of his dislike of Nazi Youth.

When Berthold was twelve years old, his father had been killed in an accident at the steel mill. The family was very poor. His mother had to go to work cleaning people's homes, but she made barely enough money to buy food for Berthold and his three younger brothers. Berthold quit school when he was fourteen to help his mother.

"Hitler boasts that he made life better for every German. He didn't help my family. My mother earned so little that we were hungry all the time. The only people who benefit from this government are Nazis," Berthold told Franz.

When Franz asked him if he went to Nazi Youth meetings, Berthold laughed. "Not me. I hate those Nazis. They have nothing better to do than beat up little boys on the street. Yesterday, I was coming home from work when I saw a gang of Nazi boys punch and kick a boy who was half their size. The boy's face was bleeding. They were beating him because he was Jewish." Berthold told Franz that he pushed his way through the crowd and picked the boy up and walked with him to his home. "They called me a Jew lover, but they did not stop me."

Franz told Berthold how he had run away from the Nazi Youth meeting and his troubles with Herr Schmidt.

"You're not the only one who does not want to be a Nazi. There are lots of us."

Berthold told him about the Edelweiss Pirates in Düsseldorf.

"We are young people who like to have fun together," he said. "We are free spirits and we don't like
being ordered around." Berthold told him about the
groups of Edelweiss Pirates in Düsseldorf. He explained
that there were similar groups in Essen, Cologne and
other industrial cities, but they called themselves by
different names. Every group had about ten or twelve
young people. "We're all working class boys and girls.
We have a lot in common." Berthold invited Franz to
come with him that evening to meet a group of Edelweiss Pirates.

Franz went with Berthold to a small café in the working class section of the city. Eight boys and two girls were
sitting around small tables talking and laughing together. The boys wore checkered shirts, short black
trousers and Edelweiss flower pins on their collars.
Berthold introduced Franz to the group.

"With us, you can be yourself," one of the boys said
to him. "We do what we want, when we want."

It feels good to be here, Franz thought to himself.
Everyone is friendly and relaxed. And no one is yelling
or giving orders. He got himself a checkered shirt, short
black trousers and an Edelweiss pin, and went to every
meeting. Every weekend the group took hikes in the
hilly countryside bordering the Rhine River. Meetings
were always lively and relaxed. Some boys brought guitars and they sang songs, talked and laughed together.
They even wrote their own songs.

A few of the boys were openly anti-Nazi. Berthold
and some of the others wrote anti-Nazi slogans on the
sidewalks and on the walls of buildings. Writing slogans
in the streets was a way to remind people that not all
Germans loved Hitler. Franz began writing slogans on

the wall of the underground walkway on his way to work in the morning.

"DOWN WITH NAZI BRUTALITY," he wrote in big white letters on the wall of the walkway. On his way home one evening, he did not see the slogan he had written that morning. It had been scrubbed away. He stopped and took the chalk out of his pocket and began to write on the wall when he saw two Nazi Youth running towards him.

Dressed in brown uniforms with swastikas on their arms, they were patrolling the walkway. "Stop or we'll shoot," one of them shouted.

Franz ran up the stairs to the exit and crossed the street. He jumped over the row of bushes that bordered the park and hid behind them. The beam of a flashlight scanned the park.

"Come out now. We know where you are," he heard one of them shout.

Franz held his breath, careful not to make a sound. They won't dare come into the park, he told himself, and squatted beneath a bush. After a few minutes, he heard one of the Nazi Youth say, "I can't see anyone." Franz heard them walk away. When it was quiet, he peered over the bush. They were gone.

Later that evening he told the other Pirates, "those Nazis are no match for us. We know every bush and hiding spot in the city," he boasted. He did not stop writing slogans.

In 1942, the British began bombing raids on German cities and life became more difficult for the Edelweiss Pirates. The Gestapo and the police called them rowdies and delinquents and began arresting them. In December 1942, the Düsseldorf Gestapo and the secret police rounded up more than one thousand young people and sent them to prisons, reform schools, psychiatric hospitals, labor and concentration camps.

News of the arrests made the Edelweiss Pirates more rebellious. They fought with Nazi Youth on the streets and offered shelter to German army deserters, escaped prisoners from concentration camps and labor camps. They cleaned out abandoned warehouses and used them as hideouts. Some Pirates began to make armed raids on military depots. Nazi officials accused them of deliberately sabotaging war production.

Franz and Berthold kept a lookout for young people who needed help. One afternoon Franz was coming home from the steel mill and saw a small thin boy drop a bag of garbage that was bigger than he was. The garbage spilled onto the street. Franz saw the boy trying to scoop up the garbage and went up to him.

"So you are a member of the slave gang. You don't have to be a slave," he whispered. "Why don't you just leave?" Before the boy could reply, he heard the boss scream and raise his fist. "He's going to beat me," the boy said in a trembling voice.

"Run!" Franz called out and pulled him by the arm. When they were a few blocks away, they stopped to rest. Franz could see how frightened the boy was.

"I live in an orphan home. But I can't go back there now. The garbage collector will tell the director that I ran away. I'll be punished real bad," the boy told him. His name was Albert and he was fourteen years old.

Albert and many other young boys worked forty-eight hours a week as garbage collectors, street sweepers or other menial laborers. Under the Nazi social welfare system, boys as young as twelve years of age were taken out of school and sent to work. Albert could barely manage to lift the heavy bags of trash.

Small and skinny for his fourteen years, Albert was the target of jokes and teasing in the home. The director of the home never tried to help him. Instead he gave Albert's tormenters special privileges. The boy who was always picking on him was the leader of the Nazi Youth club. Albert did not know how to defend himself and stopped going to the meetings. The leader reported him to the director, who took him out of school and sent him to work for a garbage collector.

"Don't worry, you don't have to go back. I know a place where you can stay and I'll take you there," Franz told him.

"But I have no money," Albert replied.

"You don't need money. We'll look after you," he told him and brought him to an abandoned warehouse. It was dark and dusty inside the warehouse. The windows were broken and covered with cardboard. Franz introduced him to four other boys who lived there. They sat on mats on the floor, eating bread and cheese.

"We didn't expect to see you today," one of the boys said to Franz.

Franz introduced Albert to the group.

"Sit down and have some food," one of the boys said. "Don't be afraid. We are all hiding from the police."

The other boys were older than Albert, but they were all runaways. One of them had been caught stealing food and running away from the police; the other three escaped from a reform school. "None of us can go out into the streets until the police stop looking for us," one of the boys explained.

"They only look for a couple of weeks and when they

stop looking for us, we can go out and live on our own," another boy said. "The Edelweiss Pirates take good care of us while we are hiding. They are hiding more than twenty boys."

"There's only one rule everyone has to obey—no stealing. If anyone is caught stealing, the police will find out about the warehouse and everyone will be arrested," Franz reminded them before he left.

The boys were friendly and one of them gave Albert a blanket. Wrapping himself in its warmth, he lay down on a mat. Running away was a good idea. He wondered why he hadn't thought of doing it before. He felt safer in the warehouse than he did in the orphan home. The next day, Franz came back with a supply of food and gave Albert a clean shirt and a sweater.

Albert wanted to help Franz. He cleaned the warehouse and made sure there was no garbage around to attract rats or mice. When Franz thought it was safe for him to go out into the streets, Albert told him he wanted to work for the Edelweiss Pirates. He volunteered to watch for the Nazi patrols while Berthold or Franz wrote slogans or brought food to the young people they were hiding. Whenever he saw a patrol, he quickly warned them.

Too young to be an Edelweiss Pirate, Albert stood guard at the café when the Pirates were meeting. One cold night, he rushed into the café to warn them that a Nazi patrol was on the street. Three Nazi Youth came into the café. One of them grabbed Albert, but Franz yanked him away. The Nazi Youth raised his fist, but Franz and the others were too quick for them.

"Are you ready for a fight?" Franz taunted them. The other Pirates stood close behind him.

"We'll be back to arrest you," the young Nazi said, and left the café.

"Those bullies only fight when they think they can win," Franz said, patting Albert on the shoulder. The next day the Gestapo arrested more than seven hundred Pirates in Düsseldorf and Cologne. Franz's group managed to avoid arrest.

The Allied bombing raids increased, covering the dark streets with the wreckage of buildings. Almost every night the sirens and the sounds of anti-aircraft guns broke the silence. One night after a raid, Albert, Franz and Berthold were walking to the café when they saw the Pirates in the street fighting with a large group of Nazi Youth. There was screaming and shouting. The gang of Nazi Youth had clubs, but the Pirates had only their fists.

Albert was thrown to the ground and two Nazi Youth began kicking him. Pain flashed through his body as they pulled him to his feet and handed him over to a policeman. Albert was pushed into a car and taken to Gestapo headquarters. His body was stiff and badly bruised, but he forced himself to sit straight and keep silent. He was determined not to give the names of his friends to the Gestapo officer interrogating him.

"You riffraff are nothing but troublemakers and you will pay the price," the officer shouted. He threatened to beat Albert until he gave the names of the other boys. Albert sat in frozen silence as the officer handed him over to another policeman. He was put in jail along with Berthold and Franz and other Pirates. Franz and Albert were sent to a juvenile work camp. Berthold, who was eighteen, was sent to a concentration camp.

The Gestapo and the Hitler Youth brought an arsenal of repressive measures against the Edelweiss Pirates.

For many Edelweiss Pirates, the pursuit ended in death. In Cologne, sixteen-year-old Bernard Schink was publicly hanged in November 1944. There were similar incidents in other German cities.

Franz was reunited with his family after the war. He heard that Berthold tried to escape from the concentration camp and was killed.

4 Kirsten

DENMARK

A Danish girl
rescues Jewish children

"I'm on my way to the hospital—today I'm going to be a clown," Kirsten told her mother as she put her yellow costume with big green polka-dots and her box of face paints into a bag. Every Saturday afternoon the sixteen-year-old girl entertained the children at the Bispebjerg Hospital in Copenhagen with her clown act or a puppet show.

Kirsten carefully painted big red circles on her cheeks and a smiling red mouth around her own pink lips. She put on her clown suit, tucked her long blonde hair inside an orange wig and stepped inside the children's ward.

"It's Silly Milly, the clown," a chorus of voices greeted her as she bounced into the room. Propped up on pillows in their beds, the children laughed and clapped their hands as the clown twirled around, did somersaults, juggled three red balls and told riddles and jokes.

"Who goes to school in the ocean?" she called out.

"I know," said a little girl with curly brown hair. "Fish have schools in the ocean."

"What tells time, but cannot speak?" Kirsten asked.

"A clock," said the same little girl.

Kirsten hopped over to the girl's bedside. "I'm going to call you Funny Bunny," she told her. "You know so many riddles."

The little girl looked at Kirsten. "My name is Stella," she whispered, and pointed to the gray-haired woman who sat next to her. "Mrs. Berger is taking me home today."

"Oh, I'm so happy for you," Kirsten said, and shook the little girl's hand. Then she whirled around, did more somersaults and juggled her balls again. When she finished her act, she bowed, blew kisses and left the ward.

Mrs. Berger stopped Kirsten in the hallway. "You made Stella so happy today. She would not leave until you finished your act."

Stella stood next to the woman and whispered, "Please ask her to come to the home."

Mrs. Berger nodded her head, "Stella and I want to invite you to come to our home. You see, I am the supervisor of a Jewish orphan home where Stella lives."

"Please come, please come," Stella looked up at Kirsten with big, pleading eyes.

"The children have so little joy in their lives." Mrs. Berger explained that the children in the home were refugees. The Danish Women's League for Peace and Freedom and the Society of Jewish Women had rescued them from Germany, Poland and Czechoslovakia when the war began.

"Some children were lucky and found homes with families, but others like Stella live in orphan homes. The children don't know if they will ever see their families again," Mrs. Berger said in a quiet voice.

"I'll be happy to come to the home," Kirsten said. Stella beamed at her and reached for her hand. For the first time she saw a smile on the little girl's face.

"Three girls and five boys live in our home. Stella is the youngest. She is seven and the oldest boy is ten," Mrs. Berger explained.

"I'll be there next Wednesday after school," Kirsten said, smiling. She never refused the opportunity to entertain children. Mrs. Berger quickly wrote down the address of the home on a small sheet of paper and gave it to Kirsten.

Kirsten found the brown house near the synagogue on Krystalgrade Street. Coming up the sidewalk, she saw Stella standing at the window. The little girl opened the door and called out, "Kirsten's here, Kirsten's here!"

Mrs. Berger showed Kirsten into the small parlor where the children were waiting, and introduced her. Everyone stood up to shake her hand. They sat down again and looked at her with solemn faces. No one spoke.

"I brought my puppets," Kirsten told them, and sat behind a small table in the middle of the room. The children watched in silence as she took her puppets out of the bag.

"These are my Viking puppets," she said. She held up each puppet and told the children its name. There was the Viking sea captain in leather trousers and blue shirt, the handsome Prince Erling in a purple cloak,

Princess Frejya in a pink silk dress, and Thrym, the ugly giant with long arms and a big round head. The puppets were made of cloth and paper and had sticks beneath their clothes.

"What are Vikings?" asked one boy. The question caught Kirsten by surprise. She had never met a Danish child who did not know about Vikings.

"Vikings lived in Denmark a long time ago," she explained. "Many were sailors who traveled to faraway places in long wooden boats. They gave each other funny nicknames like Olaf the Fat, because he had a big round tummy and Erik the Red, because he had a red beard."

Kirsten lifted her Viking sea captain, put it in a boat with a rectangular sail and spoke for the puppet. "I am the Lord of the Sea. There are no waves, no winds big enough to scare me." The boat went up and down as it sailed over ocean waves and disappeared beneath the table.

Prince Erling, Princess Frejya and the giant Thrym appeared. Thrym chased Princess Frejya around the table. Prince Erling wrestled with Thrym and the giant fell down.

"You saved me from the giant." The princess spoke in a high thin voice and danced on the table with the prince.

"The prince and princess were married and lived happily ever after," Kirsten said in her natural voice.

As soon as the play was over, the children bubbled over with questions:

"Tell us more about the Vikings."

"Did giants live in the olden days?"

"Were people scared of giants?"

"Do Vikings still live in Denmark?"

"Why aren't they here any more?"

"Did they have to fight in wars?"

"Were there Jewish Vikings?"

"Were Vikings mean like the Nazis?"

As she answered their questions, Kirsten felt more relaxed. She had been worried that the children might not be interested in her Viking puppets. When it was time to leave, Stella came up to her. "Will you show us how to make puppets, too?"

"Next week I'll bring some paper bags and cloth and we'll make puppets together," she told her.

On the following visit, they made clowns, kittens, princes and fairy princesses, German soldiers and Viking sailors with paper, glue and paints. The puppets spoke of their fears, their sadness, grief and dreams of being united with their families.

"I came to Denmark because they do not like Jews in my country," a clown with a red face declared.

"I'm scared but I'm brave," declared a Viking prince.

After they had left the table to put their puppets away, Kirsten heard one girl say, "I wish there were Vikings in Poland to protect my family."

Stella turned to Kirsten and said, "In Denmark, Jewish children are safe."

Kirsten told her mother about the children in the Jewish orphanage.

"Young children should not have to worry about being safe," her mother said. "The Germans make trouble for everyone."

Kirsten's parents, like most other Danish people, hated the Nazi occupation of their country. The Danes were allowed to govern themselves until 1943, but they dreamed of the day the Germans would be defeated. Kirsten's older brother, Jens, was eighteen and had joined the Danish Resistance.

Like other girls her age, Kirsten did not pay much attention to the growing tension in the city. The Germans did not interfere in her school and she was free to give her performances.

One afternoon, Kirsten brought her face paints, balls of wool and scraps of cloth to the home.

"We're going to have a clown parade today," she announced. She painted the children's faces and helped them make wigs out of yellow and orange wool and funny hats out of paper bags. When they had finished, eight clowns were jumping, hopping and twirling around the room.

"I'm just like Silly Milly," Stella laughed.

Mrs. Berger played the harmonica while the clowns marched up and down the stairs, beating on small drums and blowing miniature horns.

Kirsten encouraged the children to make up their own puppet shows, tell her old Jewish tales and celebrate their birthdays with clown parades.

"Your visits break up the monotony of living here," Mrs. Berger told her one afternoon. "I'm afraid of the German soldiers, so the children never leave the house except to go to the Jewish school or the synagogue," she confided.

During the summer, Kirsten planned to visit her grandparents, who lived in the country.

"We're going to miss you," a chorus of voices sang out on her last visit.

"As soon as I return to Copenhagen, I'll be back to see you again," she promised.

It was August 1943 when Kirsten came back to Copenhagen. There were German soldiers on the streets and flags with swastikas flying from the flagpoles.

"The Nazis have taken over our government. The Gestapo is here too," her father told her.

"Jens hardly comes home anymore," her mother said. "I just pray that he's safe."

"Many of the neighbors know he is in the Resistance and he does not want to put us in danger," her father added.

When school began, Kirsten discovered that her Jewish friends were no longer permitted to attend. The children at the home were restless and unhappy. Even the Viking tales about fierce warriors and brave heroes did not hold their interest.

"It is just like Poland before I left," Mrs. Berger told her. "Jewish people have to wear yellow stars."

The Jewish school was closed and Mrs. Berger kept the children in the house. "They are very frightened," she said, with tears in her eyes. The older children were remembering when they'd had to leave their parents and their homes. Albert was only six years old when they arrested his father in Poland, just before he was brought to Denmark. Another child had seen her grandparents murdered. Mrs. Berger told Kirsten that the Nazis had murdered her husband shortly before she managed to escape.

One evening late in September, Jens came home. "We've just found out that the Nazis are planning to arrest Jewish people. They are going to raid all Jewish homes on the first of October. Every Jewish person must be warned." He told them that the Danish Resistance was organizing a rescue operation to transport Jews to Sweden.

"We are planning escape routes and collecting money to pay the fishermen to take them to Sweden. Until arrangements have been made, we will hide people in hospitals, churches and private homes."

"The Jewish Home for the Aged has already been raided. They dragged the old people out of their beds and took them away in a truck," Kirsten's mother said. She was a nurse and had found out about the raid earlier in the day.

Kirsten was frightened for the children in the home. Jens told her he would arrange for the children's escape. Her mother went to the church to speak to Pastor Pedersen about hiding the children. Pastor Pedersen had given many sermons condemning the Nazis' treatment of the Jewish people; she knew he would help.

As soon as she returned from the church, she told Kirsten, "Pastor Pedersen will hide the children. Tomorrow morning, you must go to Mrs. Berger and tell her to bring them to the church. I'm going to meet with some other women and we'll bring food and clothing."

Early the next morning, Kirsten went to the orphan home. When she saw Kirsten, Mrs. Berger's eyes filled with tears.

"A neighbor came and told me to hide the children, but I don't know where to go," she sobbed. Some of the children were crying. The older boys paced around the room.

"You are all coming to my church," Kirsten announced, and turned to Mrs. Berger. "That's why I am here. I came to tell you to bring the children to the church today. Pastor Pedersen is going to hide them. Bring them as soon as you can. He is waiting for you."

Mrs. Berger wiped her eyes. "Will you come with us?" she pleaded.

Kirsten nodded. She had not planned to stay, but when she saw how frightened the children were, she knew she could not leave them.

Kirsten heard Mrs. Berger cry out, "German soldiers are standing across the street. They know this is a Jewish orphan home. They are going to arrest us. We can't leave now."

Kirsten peeked out of the window and saw the soldiers standing across the street. The church was six blocks away on the other side of Krystalgrade Street. There were no alleys to hide in.

Suddenly she had an idea. "We'll dress the children up as clowns and walk in a clown parade. If we are stopped, I'll say the children are going to put on a school play." She swallowed her fear and pretended to be calm.

Mrs. Berger trusted Kirsten. She knew the children could not stay in the house.

"The soldiers won't stay there all day. They'll be going for lunch. We'll leave as soon as they are gone," Kirsten said calmly, and turned to the children. "We are going to have a clown parade. I'll paint everyone's faces and we'll be real clowns again."

The children stared at her.

"Let's get ready. You all love to be clowns," she said in a cheerful voice.

"We don't have clown costumes," one of the children argued.

"We'll make our own costumes. We'll put our clothes

on backwards and wear scarves around our necks. If you still have the wigs you made you can wear them too." Kirsten told them to hurry.

"I'm too scared to be a clown," Stella cried.

"We are going to be very brave, even braver than Vikings," Kirsten said in her clown voice. "We are going to fool those silly German soldiers."

Mrs. Berger went to find the box of face paints Kirsten had left at the home. The children changed their clothes and came downstairs with their shirts and dresses on backwards. Kirsten painted their faces and Mrs. Berger found some scarves. A few children wore the funny hats they had made. Kirsten painted yellow and red streaks on the heads of the children who did not have a wig or a clown hat. They were ready for the parade.

Cautiously, Kirsten peered out the window. "It's almost noon," she said in a quiet voice. She did not want the children to sense the fear that was rising inside her.

As soon as the soldiers had left for lunch, Kirsten gathered the children to her.

"We're going to leave right now. Remember we are clowns and clowns smile and laugh. We must not look like we are afraid. We are going to be funny and silly."

"And very brave," Stella added.

Kirsten shepherded them out of the house and down the stairs. With their heads held high, eight small clowns jumped and hopped down the street. Mrs. Berger wore Kirsten's wig and clown hat. They were crossing Krystalgrade Street when a group of German soldiers suddenly appeared.

"Look at those silly Danes. They teach their children to be clowns," one of them sneered.

"What is this all about?" he asked Kirsten.

"Can't you see? It's a clown parade," Kirsten replied stiffly. "The children are getting ready to perform in a school play."

"Why are you on the street, instead of in school?"

Just then a policeman approached. It was Mr. Johansen, Kirsten's neighbor. He had been standing nearby and had overheard Kirsten's explanation.

"Oh, officer, I know these children. They are wonderful clowns. I can't wait to see them in the school play," he said, as he turned to Kirsten. "My son wants to join your clown group," he said in a loud voice. "Let me walk you back to the school," Mr. Johansen motioned to Kirsten. He escorted the children across the street. The soldiers turned away and did not see them enter the church instead of the school.

Pastor Pedersen quickly opened the church door and ushered them inside. "We were so worried," he said to Kirsten. "Your mother sent Mr. Johansen to look for you."

"It was a good thing too. They were stopped by German soldiers," Mr. Johansen told the pastor. He turned to Kirsten. "You sure fooled those Nazis with your clowns." He patted her on the shoulder.

Kirsten thanked him. "I'm so glad you found us. I was so frightened when the soldier stopped us."

"You children are wonderful clowns," Pastor Pedersen told them, as he showed them down the stairs to the church basement.

The basement of the church was arranged like a dormitory with mattresses and blankets in rows on the floor. A big basket of sandwiches and fruit was waiting for the children.

"Your mother came with her friends and got everything ready," Pastor Pedersen explained. "The children will be safe here until we can get them on a boat. Jens is arranging their escape."

Kirsten returned to the church later that afternoon to see how the children were doing. They seemed much calmer and showed her the games that Pastor Pedersen had given them.

"Your Pastor is like our Rabbi," Stella said happily.

"Pastor Pedersen is so kind. He made us feel welcome," Mrs. Berger told her.

A few days later, they heard from Jens that he had arranged for a fisherman in Dragor to take the children to Sweden. Dragor was a small fishing village close to Copenhagen. Kirsten's mother was collecting money from her friends to pay their way.

After school the next day, she gave Kirsten an envelope filled with money for the fisherman. Kirsten put the envelope in her paint box, placed it inside her school bag, and rode off to meet Jens in the garden of the Rosenborg castle.

Her bicycle wobbled, and as Kirsten slowed down to steady it, she heard a voice shout "Stop!" It was a German officer.

"Where are you going in such a hurry?" he asked in stilted Danish and grabbed her school bag. "You Danes think you can fool us. We don't trust you for a minute," the officer said in crude Danish.

"What are you hiding in your bag?" he growled, and dumped the contents on the street.

Afraid he would open the paint box and find the money, Kirsten got off her bike and bent down to pick it up. The officer grabbed it from her and started to open it.

"Please don't open my paint box. All my paints will spill." Kirsten forced herself to smile. "You don't want to get your nice uniform dirty," she said.

The German officer looked at her suspiciously.

"Can't you see? —it's only a paint box," she repeated. The officer hesitated and then gave her back the box.

"Oh, thank you so much. You know, paints cost a lot of money," Kirsten said, forcing herself to keep smiling as she got back on her bike.

"Don't forget your books." The German pointed to the books lying on the ground.

"How stupid of me," she said. "I forgot about them." She wanted the German to think she was dumb. "You see, I don't really like school very much," she said, as she got off her bike to pick up the books.

"The Germans think we Danes are dumb, so we act dumb. That's how we fool them," her father had told her.

The officer shook his head and walked away.

Back on her bike, Kirsten could still feel her heart pounding. She held her breath as she passed more soldiers. Kirsten pedaled her bike around the city square to the gardens of the Rosenborg castle. She kept her eyes on the road and hoped the gardens would be empty.

It was a fall afternoon and a cool wind was blowing. Kirsten parked her bike near the gardens, took her school bag and went to look for Jens. There were still a few flowers blooming. No one else was in the garden. Jens was waiting behind the statue of Hans Christian Andersen. Hugging her brother, Kirsten carefully took the paint box from her school bag and put it into the pocket of Jens's jacket.

"Oh, Jens, I feel like I'm living in a nightmare." Kirsten told him about the German officer.

"You can be thankful he understood you. Most of them don't speak Danish and they expect us to understand German," he said.

"When will the children be able to leave?" Kirsten asked.

"The children have to get to Dragor tonight. A fishing boat will be waiting at the harbor. Pastor Pedersen has already made arrangements." Jens was in a hurry to get back to Dragor. As he was leaving he turned to Kirsten. "Be careful," he warned.

When Kirsten arrived at the church, she went around to the side of the stone building and knocked on the door. Pastor Pedersen opened the door and took her inside. He told her that the children would be leaving in a milk wagon later that night.

"We have to get them out quietly. The Germans have become suspicious and have been searching some of the churches."

The light in the basement was dim. The children were sitting silently on the floor. They had already been told that they were going on a boat to Sweden.

"The escape is arranged. My friend will take you and the children to Dragor. You will all be hidden in a milk wagon," the Pastor explained to Mrs. Berger. He turned to the children and said, "Everyone must be very quiet in the wagon."

"I'm scared again. What happens if I cry?" Stella said.

Kirsten hugged her. "You are not going to cry. I'll stay with you until you leave." After a quiet supper, Kirsten reminded them of how brave they had been in the clown parade.

"Tonight you will be brave Vikings. You are going to sail on a boat," Kirsten encouraged them.

It was late in the night when the pastor's friend arrived in the milk wagon. A few of the children had fallen asleep. Mrs. Berger woke them. Kirsten gave each child a hug before they climbed into the wagon. "You are braver than the Vikings," she told them.

The pastor helped Mrs. Berger and the children into the wagon and covered them with a blanket. He emptied a sack of hay over the blankets. Jens met the children in Dragor and took them to the fishing boat. Later that day he came home to tell Kirsten that the fishing boat had arrived in Sweden and the children were safe.

After the war, some of the children tried to find their families. Those who could not find them chose to go back to Denmark to live.

Kirsten never lost her interest in acting. She went back to school and continued her performances until she graduated. Afterward, she joined a theatre troupe.

* * *

When the Nazis occupied Denmark in 1940, they allowed the Danes to govern their own country. But, fearing the growing Danish Resistance, in August 1943 they declared martial law and took control of the government. The Danish Resistance discovered their plan to deport Jews and alerted the Danish people. In less than a week, the rescue of the Jewish population of Denmark was organized and carried out.

5 Yojo

FRANCE

A Gypsy boy escorts
British pilots
across the Pyrénées

Yojo sat next to his father at the front of the Gypsy wagon. The pounding of horses' hoofs and the rattle of wheels could be heard through the trees. The narrow road was bordered by orchards filled with apple, peach and cherry trees. Yojo and his family were on their way to meet with other Gypsy families at a clearing in the woods.

An empty police car parked by the side of the road caught Yojo's attention and he leaned forward in his seat. "What is a police car doing in the woods?" he asked.

"Police cars are everywhere these days," his father said. "Don't worry. The car is empty. We'll be deep in the woods by the time the police get back." Yojo's father was a tribal elder and had organized the secret Gypsy gathering.

Yojo sat back in his seat. His father knew how to fool the police. When the family traveled, they kept to the back roads. His mother and two young brothers stayed inside the wagon. At night the family slept in the woods. Gypsies were forbidden by the fascist French government to camp or travel together. Family gatherings were secretly arranged.

"We are a proud people and do not let fear rule our lives," his father said. "This is not the first time our people have been chased from their homes." The Gypsies called themselves "Rom," "Roma" or "Romany." They came from India in the tenth century and settled in France, Italy, Spain and other European countries. "We keep our own customs, speak our own language and practice the trades our ancestors taught us," his father said proudly.

Woodcarvers, basket-makers, potters, musicians, singers, dancers, animal trainers and acrobats, the Rom maintained close family ties and called one another "brother" and "sister." They lived and traveled together and celebrated special occasions with music, dancing and storytelling.

At seventeen, Yojo was a tall, handsome boy with high cheekbones, dark brown eyes and long black hair. Like his father, he was proud to be a Rom. During the autumn, winter and early spring, Yojo and his father worked on the farms and orchards in the nearby French villages. Late spring and summer were times for traveling to family feasts and festivals throughout France, Spain, Italy and Belgium.

Yojo's family had been in Belgium when the war began. When the German bombing raids covered the Gypsy camp in thick black smoke, his father had decided to take the family back to France. Careful to keep ahead of the German army, they made their way to southern France and met up with other Rom families and continued to celebrate family gatherings and festivals.

Gypsy feasts are always happy times, Yojo thought to himself. The women dressed in long dresses with gold bracelets on their wrists. They cooked meat and vegetables over the campfire while the men in colorful shirts and scarves sat around and talked. Barefoot children raced one another around the campsite and the horses, tethered by long chains, grazed at the edge of the encampment. After a sumptuous meal, the musicians took out their violins and guitars and everyone danced.

"We'll have a wonderful feast tonight," Yojo's father said, turning the wagon onto a narrow lane at the edge of the forest. "There's no room to bring the wagon into the woods. We'll have to leave it here." Yojo's father jumped off the wagon and tied the horse to a tree. Yojo helped his mother and brothers climb out of the tall covered wagon, and helped his father carry a heavy carton of food up a steep hill to a clearing in the woods. While his mother went to greet the other women, his little brothers ran to play with the other children. Yojo went into the woods to collect firewood for the campfire.

He was picking up his last piece of wood when he heard screams and cries. He dropped his bundle, rushed to the edge of the clearing and stood behind a tree. Two policemen with guns were pushing the women and children towards a trail on the other side of the camp. Two other policemen pointed their guns at the men, who stood in a line. As Yojo stepped from behind the tree, he saw his father gesturing him to run away.

Before the policemen could turn around, Yojo darted back into the forest. He was careful not to make any noise. His stomach was knotted in fear. He felt drained and powerless. What to do? Should he go back and stay with his father? Then he remembered his father telling him, "There is no reason to wait until the sun meets the moon. Only the fish allows himself to be caught twice by the same hook."

Deep in the woods, Yojo sank to the ground. His family was in trouble and he could not help them. The police car had been a warning. The car was empty because the police were in the woods waiting for us. Yojo closed his eyes and tried to calm himself. After what seemed like a long time, he crept back to the edge of the clearing.

The camp was deserted. Pots and scraps of food littered the ground. He went down the trail to where the horses had been tethered. They were gone. Everyone—his mother, father and younger brothers, aunts, uncles and cousins—had been arrested. With a heavy heart, Yojo went back to the forest. Alone and miserable, he lay down beneath an oak tree. The ground was damp and the air was cold. He shivered. Images of the police pushing his mother and brothers filled his mind.

He was not afraid to be alone in the forest. Rom know how to find food and shelter and make ourselves at home, he told himself. But he did not want to stay in the forest; he wanted to find a way to help his people. I will search the woods for other Rom, he thought, as he made himself a bed of leaves to keep out the chill. Finally he fell asleep.

Early the next morning, as the first rays of sunlight pierced through the trees, Yojo opened his eyes and looked around. Only the chirping of a bird broke the silence. He got up and wandered through the nearby woods to see if anyone else had escaped. He found himself some roots to eat, but he found no other Rom.

Stopping at a stream, he washed his hands and face and began to walk again. The trees were thinning; he had reached the far side of the forest. Yojo could see a few farmhouses across a large field and knew that he was near the village where he and his father had worked for Gaston, a farmer who helped resistance fighters hiding from the Nazis. Yojo remembered that his father had helped Gaston deliver food to a camp hidden in the woods.

"With our knowledge of the countryside and the forests, we are a big help to the Resistance," his father told him. Gaston will help me join the Resistance. He decided to go to Gaston. It was late afternoon. Yojo waited until it was dark before he left the forest. He did not want to be seen.

The hours passed slowly. As soon as the sun went down, Yojo raced across the field to Gaston's small stone farmhouse and peered in the window. Gaston and his wife were alone. Yojo knocked on the door.

"Ah, it's my young Gypsy friend." Gaston opened the door and told Yojo to come inside. "Have you come back to work for me again?"

"My family has been arrested." Yojo clenched his hands to stop from shaking.

"I know that Gypsy camps have been raided. Your father must be very happy that you escaped," he said in a soft voice, and took Yojo into the kitchen. "You must be hungry." Gaston called his wife.

Yojo sat at the kitchen table. Gaston's wife gave him a bowl of soup and a chunk of bread. He'd just begun to eat when a knock on the door made him jump up from the chair.

"Sit down, sit down and eat. You have nothing to fear," Gaston assured him, and went to answer the door.

Yojo heard a man's voice, but could not make out what he was saying. The farmer came back to the kitchen and told Yojo, "Some British planes were shot down. The pilots are being hidden by two families in the next village. The police are searching for them."

"I should go back to the forest. It will be dangerous for you to keep me here," Yojo said.

"No, I want you to stay on the farm. I can use your help, but you can't stay here looking like a Gypsy. You need to look like a farmer." Gaston brought him a pair of blue cotton trousers and a white shirt, and asked his wife to cut Yojo's hair. He sat in the chair feeling very strange.

Clothes and hair don't make the man, Yojo told himself, as his long locks of dark hair fell to the floor. Yojo put on his farmer's clothes.

"Now you look like a real farmer," Gaston said, smiling at the tall Gypsy boy.

"Will I be able to look for other Gypsies in the village?" Yojo asked him.

"Not now." Gaston explained that Yojo would have to stay inside the house until he could get him a new identification card. Once he had a card, he could go into the village. He took Yojo up a narrow flight of stairs to the attic. A small bed filled the tiny room.

Yojo had never slept in a farmhouse before. He was used to sleeping in the open air or in the wagon. He took off his new clothes, folded them carefully, wrapped himself in a blanket and lay down on the bed. In the quiet of the room, he thought about his family. Where were they? Were they still together? Were they alive? he wondered before he fell asleep.

Early the next morning, Yojo put on his farmer's clothes and went down to the kitchen. Gaston's wife gave him a hot breakfast of eggs and freshly baked bread.

"There's lots of work to do in the house," she told him. "Time goes faster when you are busy." As soon as he was finished eating, she gave him a pail of soapy water and a mop. Yojo mopped the kitchen floor and did repairs around the house. He did not mind the work, but he was uneasy. It felt strange living in the farmhouse. Yojo knew he had no choice; he had to be patient and cooperate with the farmer and his wife who were hiding him. There was no other way, he thought, remembering his father's words, "You cannot buy what is not for sale."

A few days later, Gaston brought him an identification card with the name "René de Bruche" printed on it. "If anyone asks your name, you tell him it is René," he said.

Yojo nodded and put the card in his pocket and turned to Gaston, "Can I go into the village now?" he asked. "I want to look for my people."

"I know you do, but I need your help now," Gaston spoke in a low voice. "You speak good French and you know how to drive a wagon. The farmers who are hiding British pilots need to have food brought to them. It is too dangerous for them to go to the marketplace. They need to have it delivered to their homes," he explained.

"Who better than a Rom to bring food to hungry people," Yojo replied.

"Then you'll stay with me on the farm?" the farmer asked.

Yojo agreed to stay and help Gaston. He could look for his people when he traveled between the villages.

"I'm going to make arrangements and tomorrow you can begin to deliver packages of food," Gaston said, smiling.

Early the next morning, Yojo helped the farmer put a heavy carton of food in a small wagon and harness the horse.

"Remember to stay off the main road," Gaston warned. Yojo climbed onto the wagon and took the reins in his hands. He was happy to be on the road again. He knew he had to be careful. To keep the horse from stumbling on the stones and branches that cluttered the narrow lane, he jumped off the wagon and led the horse by its halter. The distant whirr of a motorcar kept him alert; the main road was patrolled. Only the military and the police had gas for cars and trucks.

The sound of the motorcar startled the horse and it reared, almost toppling the wagon. Yojo stroked the horse's nose to calm it as they walked. He looked for the lane that led to the farmhouse where the British pilots were being hidden.

At the farm, he tied the horse to a fence post a short distance from the house and carried the carton to the back door. He knocked on the door five times as he had been told. An elderly woman opened the door. Without a word, Yojo carried the carton into the kitchen, placed it on the table and turned to leave. The woman smiled and thanked him.

Back in the wagon again, Yojo drove slowly. It was

almost summer and the sweet fragrance in the air re-minded him of his travels with his family.

"It's the good things in life that are important," his father always said.

Yojo made three or four deliveries every week. He took food to resistance fighters hiding in the woods, as well as to farmers. When he was not delivering food, he helped Gaston on the farm.

One afternoon, he passed a tavern where he had often gone with his father. He stopped and went in. The tavern keeper recognized him.

"How is your father?" the tavern keeper asked. Yojo told him about his father's arrest and asked, "Do you know if there are any Gypsies who still live around here?"

The tavern keeper nodded and told him about a group of Gypsies hiding in an old abandoned stone building and told him where to find it.

"At last, I'm going to see some of my people," Yojo said, and made his way straight to the old building. No one was there—the building was deserted. Disap-pointed, Yojo made his way back to the farm and told Gaston he wanted to do more rescue work.

"Patience, my young friend," Gaston said. "You are doing a good job. Delivering food is rescue work."

One morning, as he was on his way to deliver a large parcel of food to a distant village, a farmer who lived down the road came running towards him, shouting, "Are you going to the village? I need a lift. I broke the wheel of my wagon and I need to do some errands."

Before Yojo could say anything, the farmer climbed up on the wagon and sat next to him. "Where are you going?" he asked.

"I'll be passing the village and I'll drop you off."

"You haven't been in the village very long, have you?" he asked. "You don't look familiar. Say, you're not a runaway Gypsy, are you?"

Remembering his father's words, "With silence, you can fool even the devil," Yojo did not reply.

"What's your name?" the farmer asked.

"René," Yojo said.

The farmer kept pressing him with questions. As soon as they reached the village, the farmer jumped off the wagon without thanking him. Yojo sensed there would soon be trouble.

When he returned to the farm later that afternoon, Gaston was waiting for him in back of the house.

"The farmer you helped this morning is telling everybody you are a runaway Gypsy," Gaston told him as soon as he had put the horse in the stable. "I'm afraid it's no longer safe for you to stay here." Yojo knew that if the farmer suspected Gaston, the whole rescue operation would be put in danger. Another British plane had been shot down and German soldiers and the French police were searching the village.

"I can go back to the forest," Yojo offered.

Gaston put his arm on his shoulder. "If you really want to help with rescue operations, now is your chance. American and British pilots are being helped to escape into Spain across the Pyrénées. They need guides."

"I know my way across the mountains. I want to be a guide."

"I thought you would. I have already made the arrangements."

"A man named Gérard is waiting for you in the tavern. Look for a man with gray hair. He's wearing a black suit and a tie with red and white stripes."

Gaston gave Yojo a wallet with some money. "We'll meet again one day, my young friend," he said, and shook Yojo's hand.

Yojo walked to the tavern and found Gérard sitting alone at a table. As soon as he saw the young Gypsy in his farmer's clothes, he got up and introduced himself. He took Yojo into a room at the back of the tavern, sat him at a table and questioned him closely. Gérard wanted to find out how much Yojo knew about the route through the Pyrénées mountains.

Yojo described the countryside, the hillsides and the vineyards that lay between the farming village and the mountains. He drew a crude map and told Gérard about his family's trips through the Pyrénées.

"You know the country very well," Gérard said, smiling. "The Germans have increased their patrols and we have to use many different routes. There are smugglers willing to take people across the mountains for a great deal of money, but I prefer to rely on someone I can trust. With the knowledge you have, you'll make a good escort."

Yojo liked the older man and was eager to get started. "Taking people across the mountains is just what I want to do," Yojo told him. This was a chance to do real rescue work.

"Two British pilots are waiting for an escort," Gérard told him. "I'll take you to meet them now," he said, getting up from the table. Gérard motioned to Yojo to follow him.

On the way to the safe house where the pilots were hiding, Gérard gave him instructions. "First you will take them to a safe house near the mountains. When you get there, you'll be given new identification papers and mountain boots. You'll need to be very careful. The safe house where you are taking the pilots is in the German zone and the area is patrolled by German soldiers."

Gérard took him to a small farmhouse on the outskirts of the village. A young woman opened the door and took them inside. Gérard introduced Yojo to Fred and Glen, the British pilots. They were dressed in farmers' clothes. The pilots came over to Yojo and shook his hand.

"Glad to meet you," they said in English. Yojo did not speak English and wondered how he was going to tell them where to go if he could not speak to them. Gérard read his thoughts.

"Not to worry," he said. "They know they have to stay close to you and follow you. When you get to the Spanish border, they will know where to go."

Gérard gave Yojo a paper with a few English phrases written on it: "Come this way," "Wait," "Hide" and "Run." He read the phrases out loud. Yojo memorized them and practiced saying them.

"When you leave the house in the morning, you'll take a wagon with the pilots hidden inside. When you get to the safe house, leave the wagon there and make the rest of the trip on foot."

The pilots kept smiling at Yojo and he smiled back, wishing he could talk to them. They ate a meal together. Very early the next morning, the young woman gave them breakfast and a bag of sandwiches and some fruit for the trip.

The pilots climbed onto the wagon. Yojo covered them with a blanket and put a pile of hay on top. Gérard put a basket of eggs and a few chickens on top of the hay and wished them a good journey.

Seated in the driver's seat, Yojo pulled on the reins and steered the wagon onto a narrow road that bordered the fields. Along the road, past abandoned farms, Yojo kept a lookout for the police patrols. It was a warm sunny day and the road was clear. When the sun was high in the sky, Yojo stopped near an empty field and helped the pilots out of the wagon. They needed to walk around and stretch their muscles. Fred and Glen followed him into the field. Yojo began to run and the pilots ran too. Then he sat down and watched to see what they would do. Fred and Glen sat down. Yojo realized that his gestures and movements would be the way to communicate with them. Sitting in the field, Yojo opened the bag and gave them each a sandwich.

He said, "Eat," in English and began to eat a sandwich. Fred laughed and took a bite of his sandwich. Glen nodded his head. Yojo knew they trusted him.

Back in the wagon again, Yojo was careful to cover the blankets with the hay and put the box of chickens on top. Flat fields merged with rolling hills and blooming vineyards. As they approached the town where the safe house was located, it began to rain. A policeman coming out of a tavern stopped Yojo and demanded to see his identification paper.

"What are you doing out in the rain?" he asked.

"Oh, just making a delivery," Yojo replied. "I'm bringing some chickens to a friend who lives here."

"I never saw a farmer deliver chickens in the rain," the policeman said. Yojo tried to smile and said in a quiet voice, "To tell the truth, I don't like making deliveries in the rain. But I promised my friend I'd bring them."

"Your chickens are getting wet," the policeman laughed, handing him back his identification card. Yojo let out a deep sigh and pulled hard on the reins. The horses started moving again. Soon they were on the outskirts of the harbor town close to the Pyrénées mountains. It was raining hard, but Yojo did not stop until they reached an old stone house at the edge of town that served as the safe house. Yojo jumped off the wagon and tethered the horse to the fence. He carried the chickens to the house and knocked on the door.

"I've come to deliver your chickens," he said to the man who opened the door.

The man nodded. "I've been expecting you," he said, and took the chickens. Yojo went back to the wagon, brushed the hay to one side and lifted the blankets. The pilots shivered as they climbed out of the wagon. Their clothes were wet. Fred turned to Yojo, grabbed his hand, shook it and made a victory sign.

Inside the house, a woman gave them towels and dry clothes. After a dinner of spicy stew and bread, the man in charge of the safe house spoke to the pilots in English. He took their pictures for fake French identity cards. Yojo handed over the card Gaston had given him. The man gave them their new cards later that night. Yojo and the pilots were also given thick woolen socks, sweaters and climbing boots with heavy spiked soles.

"The biggest risk of discovery is leaving town and beginning the climb up the mountain," he explained. "You'll be walking a few miles through the vineyards. Try to look as if you are working there. Do not walk side by side," he warned.

At breakfast early the next morning, the woman told them to eat as much as they could. "You won't be eating a real meal for a long time and carrying a bag of food will make you look suspicious," she explained, and gave them each a few apples, some bread and sugar cubes.

Yojo walked through the vineyards with the pilots trailing behind him. Careful not to look different from the other men in the vineyards, they walked slowly through the hills. When he saw the steep cliff walls bordering the road, Yojo knew they were close to the mountain path.

The main mountain road could not be used; it was patrolled by the German army and the French police. Yojo looked for the small, steep, gravelly path that ran parallel to the road and crossed the mountains. This was the path that was used by smugglers who made their way from France to Spain and back again. Yojo remembered the smugglers' road he had walked on with his father. He led the pilots through thick brush to the narrow track and they began the climb.

The green hills sloped sharply down to the sea. The road was narrow and treacherous. Yojo climbed slowly and kept looking back at Glen and Fred, who were close behind him. When Glen tripped over a rock, Yojo turned back to take his arm and guide him along the difficult trail. Near the mountain peak, the rise became more gentle.

At the top of the peak, Yojo could see the blue waters of the Mediterranean Sea. The cliffs fell away, revealing a sheet of brilliant turquoise that was the Spanish coast.

Yojo had taken them as far as he could. He pointed to the land below. It was Spain. The pilots were to go the rest of the way by themselves. Yojo shook their hands and waved to them as they climbed down the hillside. Then he turned back to the road and slowly made his way back across the Pyrénées to the safe house.

*   *   *

Yojo helped more than one hundred people escape. Many were British pilots; others were Jewish refugees or prisoners-of-war who had managed to escape from the Nazis.

After the war, Yojo located some of his aunts and uncles. They had returned to France after they were released from the Auschwitz concentration camp. There thousands of Rom men, women and children were murdered, including Yojo's own family. More than five hundred thousand Gypsies were murdered by the Nazis. The Romany word for Holocaust is *"Porraimus"*— "the Devouring."

Determined to live his life as a Rom, Yojo joined his relatives and went to live with his people.

6 Anneliese

GERMANY

An orphan girl
flees from the
German Maidens

"Run, run into the forest," Anneliese shouted. She grabbed the two youngest children and ran with them into the woods, crouching behind a bush. The German soldiers were close behind them, firing their rifles. There was screaming and crying. The shooters were relentless and bodies were scattered everywhere. Anneliese and the boys were murdered along with the other young people who lived in St. Joseph's Home in Silesia.

The Nazi officials calmly boarded the bus that was meant to rescue the children. The priest buried his head in his hands and the nuns wept.

Anneliese grew up in an orphanage for girls. She never knew her parents. The supervisor of the orphan home and the teachers at the school paid little attention to the shy, quiet girl.

"The only time I feel that anyone really cares about

me is when I'm at church," Anneliese confided to one of the nuns.

"You are a bright, wonderful girl. You must never feel that you are alone," the sister told her. She gave Anneliese books to read and encouraged her to work hard in school. Anneliese read fairy tales and stories of saints and heroes. She tried not to notice the changes that took place around her.

The small orphan home had become very crowded with newcomers, while the older girls Anneliese trusted were leaving the home. It was hard to find time for her studies, because she was given so many chores to do in the home. When the smaller girls needed help, they came to Anneliese, knowing she was always willing to assist them.

Soon after her fourteenth birthday, the supervisor insisted that she join the German Maidens. The new supervisor was a tall, stern-looking woman who made strict rules and punished the girls who did not obey her.

"No more church for you," the supervisor told her. "You'll go to the meetings with the other girls on Sundays."

Anneliese was heartbroken. Going to church was important to her, but she dared not protest. She was afraid of the supervisor.

She knew that if she did not go to the meetings, she would not be allowed to go to high school. More than anything, Anneliese wanted to finish high school—she wanted to be a teacher or a nurse. The meetings were a nuisance—they took precious time away from her books and her studies. Despite what she was told, she did not think the Germans were better than anyone else. At the meetings, Anneliese kept to herself and left as soon as she could.

Sometimes the girls had to go on marches. They chanted pro-Hitler slogans and waved Nazi flags. One day, after the march, the leader approached her.

"I notice you never sing when we are marching with the German Maidens," the leader scolded.

Anneliese turned away. She could feel a hot blush redden her cheeks. She knew better than to argue. She thought the slogans were hateful, but she kept her thoughts to herself.

"You never brag about yourself," one of the other girls told her after a meeting. "You are getting so pretty with your long blonde hair and blue eyes."

Anneliese blushed. "Looks aren't important," she said. Besides, when she looked into the mirror, she did not see a pretty face, she saw only sadness.

"Oh, I don't agree. Looks are everything. Just look at the posters. You never see an ugly person in a poster."

"I don't want to be a picture on a poster," Anneliese said quietly.

On her sixteenth birthday, the supervisor of the home told her she was to be sent to a house in the rural countryside.

"You are so lucky, Anneliese. You're going to a beautiful mansion. The German Maidens have selected you for a special assignment and you will be treated like a princess," the supervisor told her.

Why would the German Maidens choose her? she wondered. She was less than enthusiastic at the meetings.

"What will I be doing?" she asked.

"I cannot tell you what you will be doing, but you are very lucky to be chosen for this special assignment and you will be treated very well," the supervisor said curtly. "You should be grateful," she said, and ordered her to pack her belongings.

Anneliese would have preferred to finish the term at school, but she dared not argue with the supervisor. Life in the country will be much more peaceful than living here, she thought. Anneliese packed her few belongings, her books and her Bible. It might be good to work on a farm or an orchard, she told herself.

Anneliese boarded the train with one other girl from the home.

"Do you know what we'll be doing in the country?" she asked the other girl.

"No, but I don't care. It will be fun living in a mansion," the girl replied.

"I guess we'll find out what we're supposed to do when we get there," Anneliese said, and turned her attention to the sight of the rolling hills, forests and farms they could see from the train window.

There were eight other girls at the mansion. The living room was decorated with a beautiful red carpet. Large, comfortable sofas and chairs covered in colorful printed fabrics were tastefully placed around the room. Every girl had her own room. Anneliese had never seen such a pretty bedroom. The bed was also large and comfortable and a flowered curtain decorated the big window that overlooked a garden.

The girls in the home came from all over Germany. Everyone talked at once. It seemed to Anneliese that all the girls were happy. She was surprised when the girls were given pretty new dresses to wear. The meals were delicious. Anneliese had never tasted so many different kinds of food before.

In the new peaceful surroundings, Anneliese began to relax and explore the countryside. She walked in the gardens surrounding the mansion and explored the forest across the road. She still had no idea what she would be doing. There were no farms or orchards nearby. She wondered why there were no supervisors in the home. An older woman greeted the girls when they arrived, but she did not live in the mansion.

"What kind of work will we be doing?" she asked another girl.

The girl looked at Anneliese and began to laugh. "Don't you know why we are here?"

Anneliese shook her head and the girl laughed louder. "We were chosen because we are all pretty. We are here to give the soldiers a good time and we are going to make babies for Hitler." Anneliese shook her head, not believing her.

The girl was still laughing when she called the others into the room. Between loud shrieks of laughter the girl told them, "Anneliese doesn't know why she is here."

The other girls joined in the laughter. "We are going to have a good time with handsome soldiers and make beautiful babies for Hitler," they repeated. Anneliese gasped; her hands were trembling. She had heard of girls getting pregnant before they were married, but she did not want that to happen to her. She wanted to finish school.

"I'm only sixteen years old," she managed to say.

"Don't be afraid," one of the girls said. "You'll see. We are going to have a lot of fun. We'll be having parties nearly every night and besides, they treat us really well here."

"It's a privilege to make perfect babies for the Fatherland. It's your duty," another girl told her.

Anneliese went up to her room. She did not know what to do. No one can force me to do something I don't want to do, she told herself.

That night a group of soldiers came to the house and there was a party, but Anneliese pretended to be sick and did not go downstairs. The next morning she spoke to the woman who visited the house every day. "Please send me back to the orphanage," Anneliese pleaded. "I did not know why they sent me here and I want to go home."

The woman looked at her and frowned. "I am afraid I cannot do that. You were sent here to do your duty for Hitler," she snapped.

Anneliese was confused and frightened. She did not know what to do. She did not go downstairs that evening. Lying curled up in her bed, she was suddenly startled by a loud knock on the door.

"Please go away," Anneliese called out.

The door opened and a tall soldier came into the room.

"Hi, pretty girl. Aren't you glad to see me?"

Anneliese sat up quickly and held the blanket in front of her. "Don't you know I'm sick?" she whispered, fighting the deep fear that took hold of her.

The soldier frowned. "You were supposed to be my date for the night. You're not going to disappoint me."

"I'm sorry, but I'm too sick," Anneliese began to sob.

The soldier smirked at her and tried to grab her, but she quickly rolled off the bed and told him to leave. He went after her and grabbed her again and began to pull off her clothes, but she fought him off.

He laughed at her. "You don't want to make me angry,

do you?" Anneliese shook her head. She felt desperate and sick to her stomach. She thought she was going to throw up.

The soldier stared at her and turned away.

"I'll be back tomorrow. You'd better be ready for me," he said, and left the room.

Anneliese felt violated and ashamed. She had nothing; not even her body belonged to her anymore.

"The only one who can help me now is myself," she told herself as she made up her mind to run away. She lay awake all night and with the first light of dawn, she quietly left the mansion. Outside, the first rays of light were streaking across the sky as she hurried across the road to the forest. She wondered which direction to take. Saying a quiet prayer, she headed into the forest. She stepped around the bushes and trees, taking care to walk in one direction.

Sunlight streamed through the trees and Anneliese sat down to rest against a tall tree, imagining that the trees were protecting her. The thought comforted her. When she got up to walk again she noticed that the trees were thinning; she had come to the edge of the forest. Across the road, she saw a small church and ran towards it.

Sister Mary was coming out of the church and stopped when she saw the disheveled girl running towards the church. Anneliese began sobbing. It was as if all the fear inside her had exploded and she could not get her breath. The nun took Anneliese by the arm and led her into the church. When she was seated, the nun gave her a handkerchief and asked her if she was running away. Anneliese nodded and told the sister everything. She told her about the mansion where the girls were ordered to make babies for the Father-land. Sister Mary listened quietly and then took Anneliese's hand.

"You are safe now," she said. "There is no need to be afraid."

Next to the church was a small home for twenty-six children and young people. Sister Mary introduced Anneliese to Father Reiss, who told her she could stay at the home if she was willing to help take care of the boys and girls who lived there. He told her that the children had disabilities: some were mentally slow, while others had physical problems. Most of them were independent, but they needed help with schoolwork and other chores.

Anneliese nodded her head. With tears in her eyes, she told the priest, "I love children and I want to do what I can."

"You will be expected to help with cleaning and cooking chores too," he said kindly.

"I'll do anything I can." Anneliese felt as if her prayers had been answered.

Sister Mary took Anneliese to the dining room where the residents were eating breakfast. She saw boys and girls sitting around the tables. Some had crutches and others had misshapen bodies, but there was no fighting or loud talk. Anneliese saw the smiles and heard the quiet laughter and felt that she had come home after a very long journey.

Sister Mary took Anneliese to the tables and intro-duced her. One by one they stood up and greeted her politely. One of the boys invited her to sit with them and have breakfast. He filled a plate with eggs and fresh bread and handed it to her.

"Eat as much as you want," he said, smiling. Anneliese

joined them at the table and asked them their names. She paid close attention—she wanted to be sure to remember every one.

"I feel so safe here with you and these young boys and girls," she remarked to Sister Mary, who took her to a small room with a bed and a dresser.

"It's not as fancy as the mansion, but it's so much nicer," she said.

Sister Mary told her to rest, but Anneliese was eager to find out all about the school. She asked Sister Mary to take her around the grounds.

"Most of our boys work on the small farm in back of the church and the girls work inside the home," Sister Mary explained, and took her into the school room, where the younger residents were working. There was also a sewing room.

Anneliese liked everything she saw and in a very short time she settled into the routine of the home. In the mornings she worked in the kitchen helping with cooking and cleaning, and in the afternoons she helped the younger children with their schoolwork. The children and young people at St. Joseph's found a friend in Anneliese and they looked for her when they needed help. Whenever the children were ill, they could always count on Anneliese to come to their bedsides to keep them company and read them a story. She took them on picnics and outings, and played games with them.

"I love it here," Anneliese confided to Sister Mary. "I feel like I have a real family."

"We love your being here too," Sister Mary told her. "You are making life easier for everyone."

When Anneliese looked at the young people at St. Joseph's she did not see their disabilities; instead, she saw their courage and kindness. Unlike the girls in the German Maidens, these young people accepted and encouraged one another. There was no teasing or bullying.

One afternoon, black smoke surrounded the barn. One of the older boys saw the smoke coming out of the barn and called to the others. Anneliese watched in quiet admiration as the boys filled buckets with water and quickly put out the fire. Even Father Reiss and the sisters were surprised that the boys knew exactly what to do. No one panicked or refused to help. The next day, they repaired the part of the barn that was damaged.

Anneliese had been at the home for two years when news began to circulate that Germany was losing the war. Sister Mary confided to Anneliese that she was glad. "Life was good before the Nazis came, and it will be good again," she said.

Groups of soldiers and Nazi officials trying to escape from the approaching Russian army entered the village, shattering its peacefulness. Children and young people with disabilities had been safe in homes run by religious orders in rural parts of Germany. With the arrival of Nazi officers and the soldiers who stormed into the village, this was no longer true. Father Reiss told the nuns and Anneliese that the young people at St. Joseph's were not safe. Adults and even children who lived in Germany's large institutions were being murdered and the priest was worried about the children who lived in the home.

A few months before the end of the war, a public health doctor came to see Father Reiss and told him the residents were a burden on the government and were to be given a mercy death.

"That's nonsense," Father Reiss protested. "These are hard-working young people. They are not a burden on anyone."

"I have my orders from the government and you will cooperate," the doctor insisted. He then told the priest that all the young people at St. Joseph's were to be killed with injections of poison.

Father Reiss protested to the Mayor, but he refused to help.

Father Reiss was horrified. As soon as he returned to the church, he telephoned a priest in an even more remote village and begged him to help. The priest agreed and a plan was made. Father Reiss ordered a bus to evacuate the residents. The bus was to come in a few days.

Afraid that the doctor would bring his poison to the home, the two sisters and Anneliese kept the residents away. Anneliese took them for long walks in the forest and stayed there until nightfall. The abrupt change in routine evoked fear in the young residents, who sensed the danger. They were very quiet and kept close to one another.

The Russian troops were getting near; the Nazi officials knew that they would be captured and planned to escape. Fear of the Russians also made the public health doctor impatient. He was furious with Father Reiss and went to the church at all hours of the day to give the children injections. The priest arranged for the bus to come early the next Sunday morning.

The bus came early in the morning and the driver parked in front of the church. The priest gathered the young residents to pray before they boarded the bus. Anneliese was the first to come out the door when she saw a group of German soldiers running towards the church. She got the children out of the church and told them to run into the forest. She grabbed the hands of the two smallest boys and started running. The soldiers followed them and began shooting. Anneliese pulled the boys behind a bush, but a soldier saw them. She was killed, together with the twenty-six young people who lived at St. Joseph's.

Father Reiss and the sisters watched in silent horror as the Nazi officials boarded the bus to escape from the Russian army.

*　　*　　*

St. Joseph's was a small Catholic home for young people with mental and physical disabilities in a rural village close to Germany's border with Poland. It was a haven for the young people who lived there and pro-tected its young residents from being placed in large state institutions, where many thousands were mur-dered. In March 1945, the Nazis knew that Germany was losing the war, but that did not keep them from intensifying the persecution and slaughter of people with disabilities and prisoners in concentration and death camps.

7 André

FRANCE

A deaf teenager
saves an American pilot

André climbed the tree-covered hillside and stopped to rest at the top. Looking down on the sparkling waters of the Dordogne River, he saw a streak of silver twisting and turning in the sky, trailing streams of black smoke. It was a small airplane. Deaf from birth, André could not hear the anti-aircraft guns or the sound of the plane as it crashed to the ground, but he saw the smoke rising above the trees on the other side of the river.

It was the middle of a sunny afternoon in the fall of 1943. André was on his way home. He lived on a small farm in the Dordogne River Valley in the south of France. German troops had moved into the south of France and set up military posts. The French farmers resented the German troops who took their food and set up anti-aircraft munitions in their villages. German patrols in the villages were common.

André had come back to the village to live with his father after the School for the Deaf was closed by the fascist government. He and his father lived alone; his mother had died when he was a small boy. His two older brothers were in the French army and went to Algiers after the French defeat.

Seventeen years old, André still felt like a stranger in the village. No one understood his sign language. The other young people ignored him even when he tried to speak. They did not know he could read their lips. His only friend was Claude, a boy he knew from the School for the Deaf. Claude lived in a neighboring village and the two boys got together every week.

André left his home early that morning and went to see Claude after he had delivered butter and eggs to his father's friend. But Claude was not home. Disappointed, André took his time as he climbed the hills.

André saw a parachute float down and land in a tree near the bottom of the hill. A man was caught in a tangle of ropes and was swaying from a branch. André made his way down the hillside to the tree and looked up at the pilot. When the pilot saw André, he stretched out his arm. André climbed up the tree and, holding tight to a thick branch, he grabbed the pilot's arm and pulled him close to the tree so he could hold onto a branch. He freed him from the ropes and helped him climb down.

As soon as they were on the ground, the pilot began speaking. André tried to read his lips, but he could not make out the words. He knew he was not speaking French. Seeing the American insignia on the pilot's uniform, he knew the pilot was speaking English.

André pointed to his ears and shook his head to let the pilot know he could not understand him. The pilot stopped talking and took a few steps back. André wanted him to know he could trust him. There were German patrols on the road and he knew the uniform would give the pilot away. André smiled at the pilot and, pulling off his own sweater, pushed it into the pilot's hands. Then he tugged at the pilot's jacket and gestured to him to take it off.

The pilot understood his gestures and took off his jacket and put on the sweater. Then he pointed to the pilot's trousers. He motioned to the pilot to roll up the trouser bottoms. André rubbed dirt on the cuffs.

He looked at the pilot and was surprised at how young he seemed. Dressed in his sweater, he did not look much older than André and he was the same height. Happy that he was able to communicate with the young American, André grinned and pointed to the parachute that was still tangled in the tree. He climbed back up the tree and pulled the parachute out of the branches and brought it down. Rolling it up, he hid it with the pilot's jacket beneath a bush. He brushed off his hands and waved to the pilot to follow him.

André was sure his father would be willing to hide the pilot. He knew how much his father resented the German occupation. German soldiers often came to the farm to take food and left very little for his father to sell.

André gestured to the pilot; he was anxious to get moving. They had a long walk ahead of them. He knew they should avoid the main road. The route over the hills was safer from patrols.

Motioning to the pilot to follow him, André began the climb back up the hill. Turning to make sure the pilot was close behind him, he could see the worried look on his face. His eyes were wide and he kept looking around him. André waited for him to catch up and patted him on the shoulder reassuringly. "I will take you to my home." He spoke slowly, hoping the pilot would understand his words. But the pilot only nodded his head.

The tall oak trees were still full of sheltering leaves, but soon they would be leaving the hills and would have to walk on the road. The only other choice was to cross the open fields.

The road was clear for the moment. André led the way. Suddenly, he felt the pilot tug on his arm. He turned around just in time to see a car approaching. He pushed the pilot off the road. They ran into an adjacent field and lay down on the ground. The car did not stop, and after it passed, they got up cautiously.

André shook his head. The road was too dangerous, after all. It would be safer to go through the fields to the village. Picking their way over stones and weeds that covered the field took a long time. It was getting late; the sky was beginning to darken.

A small cottage stood to one side of the field. As they passed close to the cottage, the door opened and a large black dog ran out and stood in front of them, blocking their path. André could see that the dog was barking; he stopped and stood still. Calmly, he reached out his hand to pet the dog. The dog stopped barking just as an old woman was coming out of the cottage. To their relief, the woman did not seem to notice them and the dog turned and went back into the cottage. They began walking again.

The lane that led to the village was on the other side of the field. It would take them to the village square and André knew they would be seen. For the first time, he was glad that the villagers paid so little attention to him.

Still, he was afraid someone would become suspicious when they saw him with a stranger.

What would I tell them? he wondered. Then he got an idea.

No one in the village had ever seen Claude. His father's friends knew that André had a friend in the next village. If he could teach the pilot to make some signs, people would think the pilot was his deaf friend. Turning to the pilot, André began to make signs. He showed the pilot the signs for "home" and "walk" and "speak." The pilot seemed to understand and imitated his signs.

André nodded his head. He grinned and signed, "very good." Then he showed him more signs. People who are deaf need to face one another when they sign, so it would not be unusual for them to stop when they had something to say to one another.

As they walked side by side, André turned to the pilot and made a sign. The American replied with another sign. Sure that people would think the pilot was Claude, André felt confident and took him into the village.

The church, the market, an outdoor café and a bakery bordered the village square. Passing the school next to the church, André saw a group of children talking to the priest. He waved at the priest and made a sign to the pilot. The priest seemed surprised to see him, and looked closely at his companion. He called one of the older boys to him and pointed at the pilot. A few of the other children turned to look too. They stared, but André was used to people staring at him. He led the pilot through the marketplace.

A few people still lingered in the marketplace and the bakery was still open. One of the farmers he knew walked towards him. André put his arm on the pilot's shoulder and carefully pronounced the words, "This is my friend, Claude. He is deaf like me."

The farmer did not say anything, but looked the pilot over as if he were inspecting him, then walked away. Other people were staring too, but no one stopped them.

People either look away or else they stare at you when you're deaf, he thought.

The smell of freshly baked bread wafted out of the small bakery. Remembering that his father had asked him to bring home bread, he took the pilot into the bakery.

"This is my friend, Claude. He is deaf too," he said to the baker. The baker looked puzzled and pushed two loaves of bread into André's arms. He ushered them out of the bakery through the back door.

As they got close to the farm, André saw his father waiting for him. He seemed to be expecting André to bring a stranger. André saw the anxious look on his father's face as he hurried the pilot into the barn at the back of the house. He wanted to explain, but his father signed to him, "Later. We'll talk later."

André went into the house to get a blanket and some clothes for the pilot. He brought a clean shirt and a pair of trousers to the barn and helped his father make a bed of hay for the pilot. He kept glancing at his father. How did he know I was bringing the pilot home? he wondered. He had no idea how quickly news traveled in the small farming community.

He would ask his father later, André thought. He put the blanket on the hay and went back to the house. He wanted to talk to his father. But his father just shook his head and gave him a tray with a bowl of soup and some bread for the pilot. When he brought the food into the barn, the pilot was dressed in the clothes André had given him. They fit perfectly.

Now he looks like one of us, he thought to himself, watching the pilot eat. When he finished, the young man smiled at André and said something in English. Then he wrapped himself in the blanket and lay down on the hay pile. André was pleased as he took the tray back to the kitchen. "The pilot is safe now," he said, smiling at his father.

As they sat together at the kitchen table, André wanted to tell his father that he had taught the pilot some words in sign language so that people would think the pilot was Claude, but his father did not want to talk.

"You must not worry," André spoke slowly. "I showed him my signs and he is learning. People think he is Claude."

How could he make André understand that the pilot could not stay in the village, his father wondered. News traveled quickly in the small town; everyone knew that an American fighter plane had crashed. As soon as they saw André with a stranger, they whispered their suspicions to one another.

Two of their neighbors came to tell André's father about the stranger André brought into the village. The dirty uniform trousers and André's sweater were not enough of a disguise.

"If he wears my clothes, he will look like the other boys and I will have a friend," André repeated to his father, but the older man just shook his head.

After supper, a man André did not know came to the house. The man wore farmer's clothes, but André knew he was not a farmer. He tried to read his lips as he spoke to his father, but he was talking too quickly. His father took the man out to the barn. André followed and watched the man wake the pilot and talk to him.

From the way the pilot responded, André could tell the man knew how to speak English. The pilot was smiling and talking to the man. André wanted to stay in the barn, but his father told him to go back to the house.

André went to bed, but he could not sleep. Later that night, he went out to the barn. The pilot was gone and there was no sign that he had been there. André went to his father's room and woke him up.

"The pilot is gone," he said.

His father sat up in the bed and rubbed his eyes. "I know, son. He had to go to a place where he would be safe."

"He was safe here with us," André insisted.

"It was too dangerous for him to stay here. Some people cooperate with the Germans. But now the pilot is safe. He is with people who know how to help pilots escape," he explained, and told his son to go back to bed.

André felt as if he had lost a friend. "He was learning my signs. I wanted him to stay," he told his father. He felt betrayed.

Early the next morning, a big car drove up to the farm and three German soldiers wearing boots and carrying rifles burst into the house.

"We know you are hiding an American pilot," one of the soldiers shouted in bad French. The soldiers searched the house from top to bottom, opening closet doors and looking under beds. One of the soldiers went into the barn. Another soldier came close to André's father and poked him with a rifle. When he saw the soldier push his father, he stepped close to him. Afraid the soldier would hurt his son, the older man put his fingers to his lips and motioned to him to move away. André stepped back.

His father said quietly, "You can see there is no one here but me and my son."

André could not read the soldier's lips when he yelled in German to the others, "There's no one else here but this man and a deaf dummy."

When the soldiers left, André put his arms around his father and thanked him for helping the pilot escape.

After the war André received a letter from the American pilot. André's father took it to his English-speaking friend to translate:

Dear André,

I want you to know how grateful I will always be to you. You saved my life. Your father's friend brought me to a safe place and helped me escape to England. Thanks to you, I am safely home with my family. I will never forget you. You are a real hero.

> *Your friend,*
> *Steve Halliday,*
> *United States Air Force*

8 Jacob

POLAND

The true story of a
Polish Jewish boy

I was born on the eighth of May in 1926 in Parczew, a peaceful town on the banks of the Konotopa River in north central Poland. I am the youngest in my family, with four older brothers and three older sisters. My father is a tailor and had his own shop before the German army occupied our town. My family was not rich, but we were comfortable. We lived in an old brick house close to other Jewish families and the synagogue.

Before the war, Parczew had a population of ten thousand people, half of them Jewish. Jews had lived in Poland for centuries. My parents were religious and taught me to always be respectful of other people, whether or not they were Jewish. Some people in the town did not like Jews, but we had no trouble until the Germans came.

I went to the same school with other Polish children and had many friends. Tadek, a Christian boy who is a year older than me, came to live with us when his mother died. My parents made him feel like part of the family. We taught him to speak Yiddish, the language we spoke in our home.

I was thirteen years old when Germany declared war. My brothers were in the Polish army. They fought hard to keep the Germans from invading our country. The Germans bombed our cities. I'll never forget when they bombed our town. It was ten o'clock in the morning when we heard the airplanes. Everyone rushed out of their homes and ran into the fields. We lay down on the cold ground and felt the earth shake beneath us. We could see fires too, but luckily only one house was destroyed. We did not move until it was quiet.

The German army was far more powerful than ours and Poland was defeated in two weeks. The Germans declared victory and Poland was divided between Germany and Russia. Parczew was in the German zone and German soldiers came to occupy the town.

When the German army came, everyone locked their doors. My mother stocked up on food and my father closed his shop until we knew what was happening. At first the soldiers did not bother us. My father opened his shop again and people started coming out of their houses. The markets opened and life seemed normal. My brothers came home from the army and we were happy to be together again.

In the early days of the Occupation, nobody had any idea of how miserable life was to become for Jewish people and for other Polish people too. After I finished the sixth grade, Jewish children were forbidden to go to school. All Polish boys who did not go to school had to work for the German army. I went to work in the canteen for the soldiers. We worked hard for them and as long as we were willing to work, they did not bother us. In fact, some of our neighbors began to treat us worse than the soldiers.

With my light brown hair and blue eyes, I did not look different from other Polish boys. But when I saw boys I knew on the street, they turned away from me.

"What's wrong with you? Don't you remember me?" I called to one boy who had been in my class. He turned and looked at me and whispered, "It's dangerous to be with Jews. Don't you know that?"

When I started working at the *Wehrmacht* (German military) canteen, I was lonely, but I did not mind the work because I had nothing else to do. Two other Jewish boys also worked at the canteen. I worked from seven-thirty in the morning until five o'clock in the afternoon.

The *Wehrmacht* canteen occupied all the space in the school gymnasium. There were soldiers there all the time. I shined their shoes, chopped wood and went on errands for them. The *Wehrmacht* soldiers were not cruel; some were even friendly, and when I went on errands to buy cigarettes for them, I was able to buy food for my family. The army gave us official papers to prove we were workers in the canteen. Things were calm until the war against Russia began and the German SS soldiers came to the city. The SS was a special force in charge of security, with the power of life or death over civilians.

Parczew was a stop on the way to the Russian front and hundreds of German soldiers came into town on their way to the battlefields. The canteen got very crowded and we were busy all the time. The SS soldiers made no secret of their contempt for both Poles and Jews. They made Jewish people sew yellow patches shaped like the Star of David on their clothes. Whenever the SS soldiers saw our yellow stars, they were nasty and cruel.

One day, as I was on my way to do an errand for a soldier, an SS soldier stopped me. "Here, Jew-boy, shine my shoes," he ordered. I pretended not to hear him because I was on my way to do an errand for another soldier. The SS soldier pulled me by the arm and slapped my face. "When I speak to you, you obey," he shouted. "Now bend down and polish my shoes." I had no choice. I grabbed the shoe polish from the shelf and with a rag, shined his shoes. Then I backed away and left as fast as I could. I was shaking—my legs felt like they were turning to jelly. From then on I was very careful to avoid him. A few days later I saw the same SS soldier slap a Polish boy because he did not obey him fast enough.

Before too long, the Polish military police who worked for the Germans came to town. They were even worse than the Germans. I will never forget one policeman who walked around in yellow boots and had a big dog. He went into our neighbor's house and pulled the whole family out into the street. When the old grandfather tried to protect the young children, the policeman beat him with a stick. Everybody was afraid of that policeman and tried to run away as soon as they saw him.

One night, one of the Jewish boys who worked at the canteen came to my house. His face was black and blue. He told me he was not going back to the canteen. He had been beaten by an SS officer and he wanted me to go into hiding with him.

My brother warned us not to do it. "The Polish police are out looking for Jews in hiding. They know the town very well and they know every place where people are trying to hide. It is much safer to keep working at the canteen," my brother told us. I believed him and decided to stay. The boy ran away and I never saw him again.

A few weeks later, the police made all Jewish people move into the part of the city where we lived. More and more people were crowded into our neighborhood. Around the same time, my father was forced to close his shop and I lost my job at the canteen.

To make the rest of Poland "free of Jews," the Germans sent Jews from neighboring cities, towns and villages to Parczew. Hundreds of Jewish refugees came to our town. The leaders of the Jewish Council thought if they cooperated with the Germans, Jewish people would be left in peace. The refugees had to leave everything they owned behind when they left their homes, so the Parczew Jews collected food and clothing for them. Many local families took refugees into their homes.

Two families moved in with us, one from Germany and the other from a city called Jablonka in Poland. Our small house was very crowded with four more adults and six extra children. I had to share a bedroom with two of my brothers and three other boys.

My oldest brother, Isaac, was in a secret Jewish resistance group. He knew that the Germans were planning to kill all the Jews. Isaac tried to warn people and tell them how to protect themselves. Many people did not want to believe him.

One of my father's friends told him, "We Jews have lived here for generations. We helped to build this town."

"I know, but that makes no difference to the Germans," my brother said. "You'll see—things are going to get worse."

My father's friend scoffed. "This madness is only temporary. Wait and see. Things will get better for us soon," he insisted, and turned away from Isaac.

My brother knew we needed a safe hiding place and he built a very good hideout underneath the shed where we kept firewood. We all helped him dig a tunnel from the kitchen to the wood shed. Isaac put double floors beneath the shed. He put a layer of dirt between the floors so if the Germans came and tore up the floor, they would find only dirt. We had barely finished building our hiding place when German soldiers began searching Jewish homes. The soldiers came to search our house many times, but they never found our hiding place. Many Jews who were not so fortunate were arrested.

The Germans broke the treaty they had signed with Russia and attacked the Russian army. One of the leaders of the Jewish Council told us that if we helped the German army, no harm would come to us. I was one of fifty Jewish boys chosen as helpers to the German army.

Our first job was to help bring food to German soldiers on the Russian front. My mother cried when I left for the train station. She thought she would never see me again. We were put on a train to the border between Poland and Russia. At the train station, we were given big bags of hay. Twice a day, we had to feed and water the cows that were being delivered to the army camps, so the soldiers would have milk to drink and meat to eat. A German soldier gave us our orders. He was strict with us, but he was our only guard.

I boarded the train with the other boys. It was hot and stuffy inside the sealed freight cars and we had nothing to eat or drink. We had no beds and had to sleep on the floor of the train.

At the first stop, the doors opened and we jumped off the train and went to feed the cows. After we gave them hay, we filled big jugs with water at the train station so the cows could drink. When we had finished feeding and watering the cows, we had a little time to eat at the military canteen at the station. The soldier who was guarding us did not pay us close attention.

At a train station close to the Russian border, a Russian soldier approached and spoke to us. One of the boys understood Russian.

"The soldier says we should escape and join the partisans. They are fighting the Germans," the boy told us. Some of the boys wanted to try to escape. We had a good chance because we were not carefully watched. But one of the boys told the soldier who was guarding us.

The soldier stormed over to us. Furious, he warned us that if anyone escaped our families would be severely punished. We were all afraid for our families and went back to the train.

After delivering the cattle to the German army, we boarded the train again for the trip back. This time we were guarded by a group of German soldiers. At some of the train stations in Poland, I saw women, old people and children being pushed into trains. I heard them scream and cry. They were Jews being sent to concentration camps.

The German soldiers guarding us knew that we would be arrested too, if we were seen. They told us to

stay in the freight cars and be very quiet. But someone
from the SS knew that we were on the train. He came
to get us.

"We have orders to get these boys back to Parczew,"
one of the soldiers told him. The SS man shook his head,
turned around and got off the train. When we got home,
everyone was surprised that we had returned safely.

I could see that things were very bad. Only a few
hundred Jews were left in the town. People had been
forced to leave their homes and their possessions and
were taken away. The Jews that remained all lived on
one street. The street had barbed wire around it and
the Polish and Jewish guards allowed no one to leave.
My parents and sisters were hiding in our house underneath the shed, where my brother built the hiding
place. They depended on my brothers to bring them
food. One of my brothers was caught. A German soldier told him that if he were willing to work for the
Germans, he would not be harmed. My brother believed him and took me with him to work in a temporary store of the *Wehrmacht* in an old glass factory. My
job was to load blankets and other provisions into
freight trains for German soldiers on the front lines. I
had to work at the store every day, but the work was
not too hard.

I was loading a truck when a Polish policeman came
to the store with orders to bring all the Jewish workers
to the Gestapo prison. At first I did not know what to
do, but then I caught a glimpse of my brother as he was
being pushed into a truck. I started to call out to him,
but I knew I could not help him. Suddenly I didn't care
what happened, I only knew I had to get away.

I knew I had to get as far away as I could and I ran

towards the open fields on the outskirts of the town. But there was no place to hide. I spotted an old shoe polish tin and bent to pick it up.

Once I reached the field, I dug a ditch with the can. I lay down in the ditch, not knowing what else to do. It was very quiet, and I stayed there for a long time, shivering in the cold and thinking about my brother sitting in the Gestapo jail.

As soon as it was dark I left the hiding place and walked back to the city. There was no one on the streets, but I was scared and moved carefully to avoid being seen. My clothes were covered with dirt and I knew how dangerous it was to be on the streets. Then I heard footsteps and turned to run.

"Jacob, Jacob, is that you?" a voice called. I felt a wave of relief when I turned around to see my old friend, Tadek. "Come with me," he said, holding my arm. He did not seem surprised to see me coming from the fields and he took me to his house.

Once inside, he told me to sit down and gave me bread and some meat. I ate the food quickly—I was starving. Tadek knew about everything that had happened at the shop. I saw the sadness on his face and he told me that my brother, along with other Jewish workers, had been shot by the Gestapo.

I was in shock. Tadek put his arm on my shoulder. "I am so happy you escaped," he said.

"I need to go home and see my family," I told him.

"You can't leave now. It is too dangerous."

"It's dangerous for you to keep me here," I said, rising from my seat.

Tadek pushed me down onto the chair. "Your family was always good to me and I owe them a lot. I know they want you to be safe." Tadek had a plan. He was going to Germany to work with other Polish men and he wanted me to go with him.

"There are lots of Poles working in Germany now," he explained. "They need workers and they'll pay us."

"Germany is the last place I want to go," I protested.

"You have no choice," Tadek said, shaking his head. "If you stay here you will be in danger all the time. Besides, nobody will be looking for Jews in Germany."

I knew he was right. The next morning, Tadek gave me some clean trousers, a shirt and a jacket. He wasn't much bigger than I was and his clothes fit perfectly. He told me to stay in his house while he went to get me a train ticket. He came back shortly with a ticket and a false identification paper and we set off. Of course, I did not wear the yellow patch.

"You have nothing to worry about," he repeated on the way to the train station. "I've made all the arrangements. Once you get to Warsaw, my friend will meet you and show you where to go."

Tadek said that, dressed in his clothes, I looked just like all the other Polish workers. He told me again not to worry. Tadek was like a brother to me. I knew I could trust him, but I couldn't quell the cold flashes of fear in my stomach.

I got on the train and sank into a seat, not knowing what was ahead of me or if I would ever see my family again.

Tadek's friend met me at the train station in Warsaw and took me to his house. A few days later we left for Stargard in Pomerania. When we arrived, the Germans gave us an *Arbeitskarte*, a work permit. They took my picture to put on the work permit and gave me a small piece of linen with the letter "P" for Polish printed on it. I had to sew the patch of linen on the front of my shirt. It was like wearing a yellow star again.

All the Polish workers had to stand in line to have our hair cut very short. They put us in barracks and inspected our clothes. They made sure we wore our Polish patches. They did not want anyone to mistake us for Germans.

Men and boys from many different countries lived in the barracks. There were two thousand foreign workers in Stargard and I was one of them.

My biggest fear was that the other boys would discover I was Jewish. I made up my mind that I would not let myself be killed without a fight.

The privately-owned factory in Stargard was very big. Our job was to build bunkers. The foreman was a large man with a gruff voice. He could be very cruel, but he took a liking to me. "You remind me of my son," he told me. His son had been killed in the war. The foreman gave me his son's shoes and some shirts to wear. He did not hit me like he hit the others and I was grateful for that.

At sixteen, I was the youngest worker in the factory and some of the other workers felt sorry for me. Sometimes they shared their food with me. But we had little time to eat; we could only take breaks when the foreman was not around. We did not want to work hard for the Germans. One of the workers was always on guard and when he saw the foreman coming, he would signal us to get back to work.

My fear of being found out never left me. When I saw that some of the other boys received parcels from home, I saved my money and went to another barrack to buy candies. I wrapped them in a parcel and showed it to the other boys. "Look, I got some candy from my family—let's eat," I told them. I wanted them to think I got parcels just like they did.

I also wrote myself letters and mailed them from outside the barracks. It was risky to leave the barracks. I had to take the linen patch off my shirt whenever I went out. The office in the barracks posted a list of those who received mail and I waited for one of my friends to tell me my name was on the list. I made sure the other boys saw me writing letters home too.

In December of 1942, when we first arrived in Stargard, the Germans picked on Poles more than on other foreign workers. They made fun of us and called us stupid. Even children threw rocks at us. But things changed when the German army was defeated in Stalingrad. Then the Germans treated us better. We had a day off every second Sunday. I took extra jobs cleaning private houses. I wanted to save money to get back to my family.

There were very few German men in Stargard. Most of the people in town were women or old men. Most of them had nothing to do with the Polish workers, but there were a few kind people. I did not have the rationing card needed to buy food, but the woman who owned the bakery gave me bread if I came when no one else was there.

I had been in Stargard for two years when the Allies began bombing the city. Factories were destroyed and we heard that the Germans were losing the war. One of the factories had to be rebuilt. The Germans were still guarding us because they knew we did not want them to win. Among the thousands of us foreign workers, there were some who were prisoners from the concentration camps.

The Russians were coming closer and closer and even the Germans knew they were losing. They evacuated the civilian population and planned to send foreign workers to the west. The Russians got to Stargard before we could be moved. We hoped they would liberate us and let us go home. But they didn't. They moved us to another city and made us work in another factory.

When I got there I saw some boys I knew from home working in the same factory. I yearned for news of my family, but they did not know anything about them.

The day the Russians gave us permission to go home, I packed my few belongings and hurried to the train station. When I got back to Poland, I found my mother and two of my brothers still living in the house. Two of my sisters had also survived with the help of some Polish friends. My grandparents, two of my brothers and one sister had been murdered. My happiness at returning home was mixed with sorrow.

Even after the war, life was difficult for Jewish people in Poland. The peasants stole our possessions, occupied our houses and took our lands. People were desperately poor and there were bands of robbers everywhere. In 1948, with the help of an international Jewish agency, I escaped to Israel with my remaining family.

*   *   *

Jacob's story is based on the testimony a young man gave to the Yad Vashem, the Holocaust Memorial in Israel, when he arrived there in 1948.

The German occupation of Poland was brutal. The country was turned into a killing field. Many prisons were built in Poland, including three of the most notorious death camps—Majdanek, Treblinka and Auschwitz.

9 Noni

GERMANY

Escape from certain
death in Hadamar,
a German psychiatric hospital

The long, narrow ward in the state institution was eerily silent. The only sounds were the footsteps of the nurses as they hurried about the room. Noni stood alone at the dusty window watching a tiny bird fly to its nest in a tall tree. She heard the nurses whisper to one another.

"The bus from Hadamar is here now. The girls are dressed and ready to be moved."

"Have you heard the rumors about Hadamar? They have a gas chamber there. I'm afraid these girls are being sent there to die."

Hadamar was a large psychiatric hospital in northern Germany.

"I know, but we have to obey orders. There's nothing we can do about it." The nurse shrugged her shoulders and went to dress another girl.

The nurses' words filled Noni with terror. Clenching her hands to keep from trembling, she looked out of the window again and saw the big gray bus with blackened windows. She knew she was being sent away because she could not do heavy work.

Noni was sixteen years old; she was small and frail and her spine was slightly crooked, but she was not as disabled as some of the other girls on the ward. Tears filled her eyes. Nobody here cares what happens to us, she thought. Noni turned back to the window just as the tiny bird left its nest and soared up to the sky.

"If I were a bird, I would be free," she told herself. "I can't fly, but I can walk." Noni took a deep breath. She did not know how she would escape from the bus, but she was determined to try.

Noni turned from the window just as the director of the institution came into the ward with three German soldiers.

"You'll have to carry the ones who cannot walk," he said loudly, and without looking around him, he left the room.

The soldiers began to pull girls out of their wheelchairs and carry them outside.

"Get into the line," one of the soldiers shouted at Noni.

Noni joined the other girls. A soldier stood at the back of the line and prodded them outside. They stood in a line and one by one the girls climbed into the waiting bus. Close to the entrance of the bus, Noni took a deep breath. She raised her head, stepped out of the line, quickly walked around the bus and made a dash for the back of the building.

The door to the garbage shed was open. Noni entered and hid behind the big garbage bin. The stench filled her nostrils and made her gag; she swallowed hard. It was hot and airless inside the shed. She could barely breathe. Her heart was beating fast and she was dizzy with fear. Then she remembered her grandmother telling her, "Trust yourself, Noni. You may be small, but you are smart and brave. You will know what is right for you to do."

Thinking about her grandmother calmed her. Her mother died when Noni was a small girl and her father took her to live in a small farming village with her grandmother. Because she was slow to walk and talk, the village doctor told the older woman that Noni was mentally handicapped and should be put in an institution. Her grandmother did not believe him—she treated her like a normal child. When the village school refused to admit her, her grandmother taught her to read and write at home.

Noni remembered how sad and frightened she had been when her grandmother died. Her father did not come to get her. Instead, a social worker took her to a Catholic Home for children with disabilities. At first, Noni was so frightened that she would not even speak. Sister Kati, a young nun who looked after the children in the home, understood her fear. She sat by Noni's bed at night and held her hand until she fell asleep. With the sister's encouragement, Noni regained her confidence and began to speak again. She settled into life at the home and went to school again.

Shivering silently in the damp garbage shed, Noni tried to calm her fears. Sister Kati told me that I am smart and can do anything I really want to do, she reminded herself. Her memories of Sister Kati were comforting. The young nun told the children stories and taught them songs and she always carried seeds in her pockets so they could feed the birds when they went for walks.

After the Nazi authorities had closed the Catholic Home, Noni was sent to a large institution. From the moment she arrived, Noni knew her life was going to be difficult. The old stone castle had been converted into an institution. It was a cold and uncaring place. Noni's clothes and books were taken away, her hair cut short and she was given an ugly blue cotton smock to wear. The institution was crowded. The girls had to sleep in a large dormitory on narrow cots. They ate their meals in a large dining hall and there was never enough food. Every day they ate potatoes and turnips. No talking or laughing was permitted in the dining room.

Noni felt that no one cared about her anymore. It was dangerous not to obey the strict rules and she tried hard to do the work so she would not draw attention to herself. Assigned to work in the laundry, she carried heavy bags of soiled clothing and sheets to the big, steamy laundry room and brought clean laundry back up to the wards.

Her back had never been strong, and because of the laundry chores, it had begun to ache. One morning her back hurt so much she could not get out of bed. She was moved to the ward for girls who could not work. After a few weeks, Noni was able to get out of bed and walk again. But she was now considered "severely handicapped" and had to stay on the ward.

Noni realized that she had not been followed into the shed. She got up and peered outside. Seeing no one, she left the shed and made her way down the steep path that led to the road.

It was a warm spring day and without a coat or sweater

to cover up the blue smock, Noni was afraid she would be quickly recognized as a runaway from the institution. Noni was careful to stay behind the trees that bordered the road. Whenever she heard a car or truck approach, she ducked behind a tree. Her back was aching, but she did not stop to rest.

I'm free now, like the little bird, she told herself.

The road led through a small village. There was a market behind the trees and Noni went inside. Barrels filled with red and green apples, potatoes and onions were all around her. She had not eaten all day and was very hungry. She stepped up to a barrel filled with red apples and reached for one. Then she remembered her grandmother telling her never to take food unless she could pay for it. She had no money and put the apple back.

A half-eaten apple lay on the ground. Noni picked it up and began to eat it. Two small boys standing nearby watched her. One of them pointed at her and began to laugh. Noni quickly turned and went back out to the road.

She came to a large park and saw a crowd of people watching a juggler toss red, green and blue balls into the air. Noni joined the crowd. She could not take her eyes off the little colored balls that seemed to dance in the air. When the juggler had finished, the crowd scattered. Noni stayed and watched the juggler put the balls into a canvas bag. The juggler came towards her and started to speak, but she was too scared to talk to him and walked away.

Hungry and tired, she lay down beneath a tree to rest. She did not see the old woman coming towards her. The woman grabbed her arm. "Girl, help me carry these sacks to my cottage. It's not far from here," she said. Noni scrambled to her feet and tried to pull away, but the woman would not let go of her.

"Don't be afraid—I'm not going to hurt you. Can't you see—I need your help. Help me carry my bundles and I'll give you something to eat." The woman pushed two bags into her arms. Noni took them and followed the woman to a small cottage by the side of the road. The woman opened the door and stepped into the small kitchen.

"Put the bags on the table," the woman said, looking at her. "I can see from your blue frock that you come from the institution. Did you run away?"

Noni's eyes filled with tears. "Don't take me back," she pleaded. "I ran away because I did not want to go on the bus to Hadamar. I don't want to die."

"Don't worry. I won't make you go back," the woman spoke softly. "It's a terrible place. I know about Hadamar. You were smart to run away. You can stay with me tonight and help me make our supper," she said.

Noni wiped her eyes. "I am glad to help you. I know how to peel and cut potatoes and carrots." The woman smiled and took the vegetables out of the bag and washed them in a pail of water. She gave them to Noni with a small knife. Noni peeled and sliced the vegetables carefully and put them in the pot of boiling water. While the soup was cooking, she took a broom and swept the floor.

When the soup was ready, the woman motioned to her to come to the table. "You must be hungry," she said, and gave Noni a big bowl of soup and two slices of bread. Noni was very hungry and ate quickly. The woman ladled more soup into her bowl.

After dinner, the woman fell asleep in a big red arm-chair. Careful not to wake her, Noni washed the bowls and spoons and dried them. When she finished, she lay down on the floor and fell asleep.

Early the next morning, the woman woke her and gave her some bread with cheese and a cup of tea.

"Please, can I stay with you?" Noni smiled at the woman. "I'll work hard for you. I am slow, but I am not stupid."

The woman shook her head. "I can see you are a good worker, but it is better for you to get away from here. You can find work on a farm." The woman gave her a black cotton skirt, a blouse and a sweater and told her to change her clothes. The skirt and sweater were much too big for her small body. The woman trimmed the skirt with a pair of scissors and tied a cord around Noni's waist to hold the skirt up.

"Now, no one will know you're from the institution," she said. "Go back to the road and you will come to a small farming village. Farmers always need good work-ers. Tell them you will work for food and a place to sleep," she told her, and gave her a bag with fruit and some bread.

Back on the road, Noni followed the directions the woman had given her. She stopped to wash her hands and face in the cool water of a small stream near a quiet forest. She ate some fruit and bread from her bag.

She hadn't walked far again when she saw a small farm at the side of the road. A farmer was working in the field. Noni crossed the field and spoke to the farmer. "I'm looking for work. I work hard. I only ask for food and a place to sleep," she told him.

The farmer turned to look at her. He did not know

what to make of the small girl in clothes that were far too big for her. "Where do you come from?" he asked.

"I live not far from here." Noni lowered her head.

"You don't look old enough to work." The farmer kept his gaze on her. "You're not running away from home, are you?" he asked.

"I'm sixteen. You see, my grandmother got sick and died. I did not run away, but I have no home now. That's why I have to work," Noni replied.

The farmer felt sorry for her. "Who is your grandmother?" he asked in a softer voice.

"Her name is Noni, just like me," she answered. "I will work hard. I only want something to eat and some place to rest."

"I don't know any woman called Noni." The farmer nodded at her. "Come with me. I will take you to my wife and see if she has work for you."

The farmer took her to the small farmhouse and called his wife. A short, stout woman with a friendly face told Noni to come inside.

"I am a good worker. I ask only for food and a place to sleep." Noni spoke quietly. "My grandmother died and I have nowhere to go."

The farmer's wife smiled at her. "Well, I could use some help," she said, and gave Noni a pail of soapy water and a scrub brush. Noni scrubbed the kitchen floor as hard as she could. Then she washed and dried the dishes.

"You are a good worker." The farmer's wife was pleased. "Now you can rest and join my husband and me for supper."

After a meal of potato soup and bread, the farmer's wife gave Noni a blanket and sent her to the barn to sleep. She made herself a bed with a pile of hay and wrapped herself in the blanket. I'm safe now, she thought, before she fell asleep. In the morning she went back to the house.

The farmer and his wife were eating breakfast. "Good morning to you," the farmer's wife greeted her, and gave her a plate. "Help yourself," she said. Noni was careful to take a modest portion of eggs and a slice of bread. She did not want the farmer's wife to think she was greedy. "You are good to me," she said gratefully.

After breakfast, while Noni was washing the dishes, a neighbor woman came into the kitchen. "Who is that girl?" she asked.

"She is Noni; she is my new helper. Her grandmother died and she came to us looking for work," the farmer's wife replied.

"Are you sure she isn't a runaway? She doesn't look old enough to work." The woman stared at Noni. Her short hair and ill-fitting clothes made the woman suspicious. She turned to the farmer's wife and said in a loud voice, "The girl looks like a runaway from a reform school. You should call the police," the woman insisted. "You'll be in trouble if you keep her here," the woman said, and left the house.

The farmer's wife called her husband and told him what the neighbor said. The farmer asked Noni if she had run away from a reform school. Noni tried to blink back the tears that flooded her eyes, but she couldn't. The farmer's wife put her arms around her. "It's all right. You can tell us the truth. We won't report you."

Between sobs, Noni told them how she had run away from the bus. "They kill people like me at Hadamar. I do not want to die."

"We can't keep her here," the farmer told his wife. He was afraid their neighbor would report them. "We don't want trouble from the police," he said. His voice was gentle but his words were harsh. "You can't stay here," he told Noni.

The farmer's wife felt sorry for the frightened girl. She gave her a new sweater and a skirt that fit her. Noni changed her clothes again. "You look much better now." She smiled at Noni and gave her a comb and brush, a purse with a few coins in it and a bag of food. She gave her directions to a friend's farm in the next village. "You'll find work there," she told her.

Noni found the farm and knocked on the door of the farmhouse. A boy opened the door and looked at her. "We don't want beggars here," he said, and slammed the door. Noni was too frightened to knock on the door again and went back to the road.

After a while, her back began to ache again, and she sat down to rest beside a pond. It was late in the afternoon. She watched a family of tiny ducks swimming in a straight line behind their mother. One duck was swimming by itself. I'm like that duck—all alone, she thought, not knowing what to do. She wrapped the sweater around her and lay down beside the pond.

I did not get on the bus, she told herself. I am far away from the institution and I am free. A feeling of calm washed over her. She would rest and begin to search for another farm in the morning. Somewhere, she would find a new home, she thought, as she fell asleep.

The next morning, Noni brushed her hair and went to look for another farm. A woman holding a crying infant stood in front of a small farmhouse on the side of the road. Noni went up to her and told her she was looking for work.

"My husband was wounded in the war and is not able to work. We have no money to pay you," she told her.

Noni smiled at her. "You do not need to give me money. I only want food and somewhere to sleep."

"Then you can work for me. I have three small children and too much work to do. I need lots of help," the woman said, smiling, and invited Noni into the house. The tiny house was cluttered. There were clothes and papers on the floor and dishes piled in the sink. Two small children were playing on the floor. The woman's husband sat in a wheelchair.

The woman introduced Noni. After she told her husband that Noni was only asking for food and a place to stay, he welcomed her warmly.

"Look at this messy house; my wife needs your help," he said, with a warm smile. Noni knew she was safe.

After her chores, Noni played with the children and felt like part of the family. She stayed on the farm until the war was over. After the war, Noni went back to the Catholic Home and worked with Sister Kati.

*   *   *

The killing program at Hadamar, in Germany, was one of six programs called "Operation T-4." Doctors and nurses in psychiatric hospitals and state institutions carried out the killing programs. Starvation and poison injections were used, but the method of choice was gassing with carbon monoxide. Hadamar was a major killing center. In 1941, the gas chambers were moved to the death camps and administered by the same physicians who had murdered people at Hadamar and the other institutions. The killings continued. More than a quarter of a million people with physical or mental disabilities were murdered.

10 The Helmuth Huebener Group

GERMANY

The true story of three
heroic young Mormons

Helmuth stood inside the entranceway of the old apartment building waiting for his friend, Karl. As soon as he arrived, Helmuth opened the door and hustled him into the dark hallway.

"What took you so long? I was getting worried," he said.

"The streets are so dark. The lampposts are not lit. I was sure I'd be stopped by the police or get caught in an air raid," Karl murmured. The British had begun bombing attacks on Hamburg, the large northern port city.

"What's so important? Why did you want me to come so late?" Karl was breathless. He had run nearly all the way.

Helmuth put his finger to his lips. "Let's not talk here," he whispered, and took him up the stairs. "My grandparents are sleeping. We'll need to be quiet," he said. He led Karl to the kitchen at the back of the flat. Helmuth pointed to a small radio on the kitchen table.

"My brother brought it back from France; he was there with the National Labor Service," he said, grinning.

"You wanted me to come all this way to see a radio," Karl said, and plumped down on a chair.

"It has short wave. I wanted you to hear the broadcast from London," Helmuth explained, turning off the light.

"Man, are you crazy? Don't you know it's strictly forbidden to listen to foreign broadcasts?" Karl whispered.

"Nobody can hear us—now just listen." Helmuth switched on the radio. A dim light illuminated the dial. At first, all they could hear was a buzzing noise. Then in clear German a voice announced, "The BBC London presents the news in German."

They heard a long, detailed report about the fighting in Russia. The British reported that the German army had lost thousands of men in Russia; they were not winning all the battles in Africa; and the British warship, the *Royal Oak*, had not been sunk. Everything they heard contradicted the reports of the German news service.

When the program was over, Helmuth turned off the radio. "Those gentlemen in Berlin are deceiving us," he whispered. "They tell us that the army is winning the battles in Russia and Africa. The people of this country have no idea what is really happening."

Karl nodded. "I'm not surprised. I never believe what the Nazis say, but there's nothing we can do about it. I hope you haven't told anyone else that you listen to these British broadcasts."

"Only Rudi. There's no one else I can trust," Helmuth told him.

Helmuth, Karl and Rudi were members of St. Georg's,

a branch of the Mormon church in Hamburg. The boys had a lot in common, having grown up together in a working class neighborhood in the port city in the northwest corner of Germany. They saw for themselves how the city had changed after the Nazis took over. Hamburg had been a stronghold of social democracy in Germany. It took longer for the Nazis to bring Hamburg under their control than other cities in Germany. They dismantled the trade unions and the German police patrolled the working class sections of the city to prevent protest demonstrations. Young people were required to join Nazi youth groups and shops owned by Jewish people were destroyed. Karl worked in the homes and shops of Jewish people. People he liked and respected had been arrested and sent away. Rudi got into fights with the Nazi Youth.

Karl was a year older than Helmuth, but he admired the sixteen-year-old boy and jokingly called him "The Professor." Helmuth could talk about many different subjects. He was always reading books and was the youngest deacon at the church. He worked for the Hamburg city social welfare department and was a busy volunteer at the church. Herr Zander, the president of the church, gave Helmuth letters to type to the soldiers at the front. There were so many that he gave Helmuth a typewriter and paper to take home with him.

Karl was seventeen and a painter's apprentice. Rudi was the youngest; he was fifteen and worked for a mechanic. Helmuth, Rudi and Karl called themselves "The Three Musketeers," and saw one another often at the church. They didn't like some of the changes they saw in the church. Herr Zander had joined the Nazi party and put a sign on the door forbidding Jews to enter.

He wanted to bring a radio to church so the young people could listen to Hitler's speeches, but Karl's father protested, "This is a church, a place to learn about religion, not politics." The president did not bring the radio to the church, but he encouraged the young people to join the Nazi youth groups.

Karl and Rudi avoided going to Nazi Youth meetings. They worked late in the afternoons or evenings and had a good excuse. Helmuth moved into his grandparents' home to avoid fighting with his stepfather, a member of the Nazi party. He did go to some of the meetings and joked about them with his friends. "I try to keep quiet and sit there like a mummy."

"You can sit and not talk? I can't believe it," Karl laughed. Helmuth was a great talker and had opinions about everything. Some of the older members of the church thought he was arrogant, but Karl knew he was better informed than most people. The boys met at a small café after church meetings when they wanted to talk. It was not safe to speak freely at the church any more.

When the radio program ended, Karl got up from his chair. "It's really late—I'd better go now," he said.

"I have something else to show you," Helmuth said, and handed him a sheet of red paper. The words seemed to jump off the page:

Down with Hitler.
People's Seducer
People's Corrupter
People's Traitor
Down with Hitler.

"Who wrote this?" Karl asked, but he knew the answer.

"That's the first leaflet I wrote. I put copies on the bulletin boards in entranceways of apartment houses." He told Karl he'd distributed six leaflets.

"That's even crazier than listening to British broadcasts," Karl said, staring at him.

"Don't you think people have the right to know the truth? Hitler is ruining the country. Think about it. Germany has no raw materials and is dependent on other countries. The British are already bombing our cities. When the Allies get the upper hand, Germany will have nothing," Helmuth said, and gave Karl another paper. "I wrote this one just before you came."

Who is Lying ?????????

The official report of the
German High Command
of the Armed Forces.
Quite a while ago they claimed
the roads to Moscow, Kiev
and Leningrad were opened.
And today—six weeks after
Germany's invasion of the USSR—
severe battles are still occurring
far from these places.
This is how they are lying to us!

Helmuth gave Karl seven leaflets. "Will you put these in the entranceways of apartment houses on your way home?" he asked.

Karl felt a shock of fear and shook his head.

"It's easy. You don't have to put them on bulletin boards, just push them into the telephone boxes," Helmuth reassured him. "Just be careful no one sees you."

Karl left the apartment building with the leaflets. At least it's dark and there's no one around, he told himself, stopping at the door of a big apartment building. He looked around him before he went inside and pushed a leaflet into the telephone box. There were only seven leaflets, but he felt as if there were a hundred. When he delivered the last one, he took a deep breath. His legs felt weak as he hurried the rest of the way to his home.

Two policemen were standing in the entrance of the building where he lived. Karl was afraid they were waiting for him. A stab of icy fear shot through his body as he stepped in front of the policemen to open the door.

"Where are you coming from so late at night?" one of the policeman asked.

"Oh, I was just visiting a friend," Karl replied, as calmly as he could.

"Well, good night, then. Let's hope there will be no more air raids," the policeman said.

"You have a good night, too," Karl replied, and hurried inside.

Opening the door to his home, Karl felt so weak he almost sank to his knees. He was sure that if Helmuth had asked him at that moment to distribute more leaflets, he would have refused. In the morning, though, he felt better and thought he might be willing to distribute a few leaflets now and again. He knew he had taken a great risk and did not tell his mother about the leaflets.

A few days later, Helmuth saw Karl at church and

asked, "Well, how's it going? If I know you, you did every-thing perfectly."

Rudi saw his friends laughing together. "What's so funny?" he asked.

"We'll tell you later. Let's meet in the café after the church meeting," Helmuth suggested.

Karl was surprised to learn that Rudi had also delivered leaflets.

"Do you really think your little leaflets are going to convince people that they are being lied to?" Karl asked Helmuth.

"Not the little ones. I have a better plan. I want to print out the British news reports and distribute them. I'll only write a leaflet when there is something of importance," Helmuth told him.

Karl and Rudi both came to Helmuth's apartment to listen to British broadcasts on Friday or Saturday nights. To Karl's relief, Helmuth did not mention any more leaflets.

The British report their own losses as well as ours, the boys observed. They were convinced the reports were truthful. When the Russians were victorious in a major battle, Helmuth decided it was time to start a real information campaign.

"Most people do not have short wave radios and unless we tell them what is happening, they will never know," he said, and told Rudi and Karl his plan. He wanted to write a new leaflet every week to report the news they heard. Whenever he listened to a broadcast, he took notes in shorthand and typed them out, using carbon paper to make several copies. Karl and Rudi were impressed with the professional-looking leaflets.

"Who else knows about these leaflets?" Karl asked.

"No one, only the three of us and Gerhardt, my friend at work," Helmuth explained. Gerhardt was an apprentice clerk who worked with Helmuth in the city department.

Helmuth organized the distribution and assigned everyone a district where he would distribute the leaflets.

"If we get caught, we each take the blame for the whole distribution," he told them. The other boys solemnly agreed. They would never reveal the names of the others. Helmuth, Karl and Rudi continued to meet at the church. Whenever a new leaflet was ready, Helmuth signaled the others by saying, "Isn't it time for us to get together?"

Every week there was a new leaflet. When there was more news, Helmuth managed to print two in a week. The boys were distributing from sixty to one hundred and twenty leaflets every week. Helmuth found a stamp with an eagle and a swastika and stamped every leaflet so it looked as if it were a Nazi leaflet. The leaflets were tacked to bulletin boards in the entranceways of apartment buildings in all the working class sections of Hamburg.

Wandering about the dark city, they were careful not to be seen. Karl never brought the leaflets home. If he could not distribute them, he tore them into small pieces and got rid of them. Rudi was less careful. During the day he kept the leaflets in a secret hiding place behind a strip of wallpaper that had become loose. When he was ready to leave work, he took the leaflets and distributed them on his way home. He did not always wait until dark.

Karl almost got into trouble when he was chatting with friends in a neighborhood café and showed them a leaflet. They were shocked and scolded him. Grinning,

Karl told them it was a joke and put the leaflet away. From then on, he did not take any chances.

Distributing the leaflets was dangerous work; they never knew if they would be seen or reported. The mood of the city grew even more strained. The air raids had increased and many buildings were destroyed. Nazi patrols were always on guard, but Helmuth was sure they would not be caught.

In 1942, French prisoners of war were forced to work in the factories of Hamburg. Helmuth thought that, being far from their homes and forced to work for the Germans, their spirits would be buoyed by the leaflets. One of the apprentices in the city department spoke French. Helmuth gave him a leaflet and asked him to translate it into French. The apprentice read the leaflet and threw it back at Helmuth. That night, two Gestapo officers came to his grandparents' apartment and searched his room. They found the leaflets, the paper and the typewriter, and arrested Helmuth.

The following Monday, Karl was arrested and put in a green paddy wagon with twenty other prisoners. Rudi and Gerhardt were arrested a few days later. They were in the same jail, but they were not allowed to see one another. Despite the rough treatment and the cruelty of the guards, not one of them betrayed the others.

The first time Karl caught sight of Helmuth, he was horrified. Helmuth had been badly beaten—there were black and blue marks all over his face. Helmuth looked at Karl and winked. Karl was shocked and steeled himself, afraid he would go to pieces. Rudi tried to be cheerful and ignored the taunts of the guards and the harshness of prison life. Among the prisoners were physicians, scientists and teachers, as well as workers.

What they did for a living did not matter; they were all treated the same in prison.

At five o'clock in the morning the prisoners were awakened. After breakfast they were chained together and taken back to Gestapo headquarters in the paddy wagon.

The four boys had to stand trial. Throughout the proceedings, Helmuth stood tall and answered the questions truthfully. At the end of the trial, their sentences were read out loud. Gerhardt received four years' imprisonment, Karl five years, Rudi ten and Helmuth was sentenced to death.

Helmuth stood up in the courtroom. "You have sentenced me to die, even though I have committed no crime. But I must tell you that your turn will come. Germany will lose the war." Karl was amazed at his courage.

Everyone was silent as the four boys were led out of the courtroom. Karl, Rudi and Gerhardt were sent to slave labor camps in Poland and Russia. Helmuth Huebener was seventeen years old when he was executed by guillotine. He was the youngest resistance fighter to lose his life in Ploetzensee, the infamous Nazi center of death.

*   *   *

After the war, Karl-Heinz Schnibbe gave detailed testimony about the work of the Huebener group. The documents and testimonies can be read in the book *When Truth Was Treason.*

11 Karl
GERMANY

A boy with disabilities
escapes imprisonment
and finds refuge

Family, friends, neighbors and the village priest watched in silent horror as the public health official pushed Karl into the car. His mother and sister were weeping; his father called out, "Be brave, my son, you will soon be home again."

No one could understand why Karl had to go to a state institution. They knew he was a little slow and his speech was slurred, but no one thought of the friendly fifteen-year-old boy with curly blonde hair and bright blue eyes as being different. He helped his father on the farm, took eggs and butter to his neighbors and never made trouble.

When Karl's father learned that the public health official would be coming for Karl, he'd gone to the district public health office to protest.

"What possible harm is there in keeping my son at home? He is a good worker and helps me on the farm," he told the official.

"Mental defectives are a burden to the country. We have orders from the government to remove feeble-minded people from the community," the official said coldly.

"My son is not feeble-minded. He is not a burden on anyone," Karl's father insisted. "Who told you he is feeble-minded?"

"We have a report from your village doctor," the official replied. "He wrote that your son has a mental handicap."

The village doctor knew Karl. How could he say that? Karl's father was furious.

Failure to report people with disabilities was punishable under Nazi law. The doctor was afraid he would be punished and filed a report on Karl. He never thought that his report would be used to take the boy with a mild mental handicap from his home.

The public health official handed Karl's father a paper to sign. It gave the official the authority to take Karl to the state institution. Karl's father refused to sign the paper. "I won't let you take him away," he told the official.

"You don't have a choice," the official said. "Get your son ready. We'll be coming for him soon." Karl's father hurried out of the office. As soon as he got home, he and his wife went to the village priest and told the neighbors that Karl was going to be taken away. He did not know what else to do.

The next day, the public health official arrived and waved an official document at Karl's father. "I have orders to take your son today," he said in a loud voice.

"I told you I will not sign the form. You cannot take him," Karl's father replied and tried to close the door.

The official held the door open. "I have orders to take your son. You have no choice. You will let me take him now or I'll call the police and arrest him. I'll arrest you too. Your son cannot stay in the village," the public health official shouted.

His father realized there was nothing he could do. He felt helpless and defeated. He did not want the police to come. He asked the official to wait while, trembling with fear and anger, he went to get Karl.

When the neighbors saw the official's car, they knew Karl was to be taken away. They gathered in front of the little farmhouse and waited. The village priest joined them.

Karl knew he would have to go to the state institution. He had heard his father talking to the neighbors and he heard the official threaten his father. To his father's surprise, Karl understood that he had to leave. He did not want to make trouble for his family. "I don't want you to go to jail, Papa," he said quietly.

"We love you, son. We'll do everything we can to bring you home soon." His father put his arm around him and led him outside. His mother wept as she handed him a small suitcase.

The public health official told Karl's parents, "Don't worry. He will be well looked after in the institution. They know how to take care of these people." He took Karl to the car. "Don't worry son, you'll be home soon," his father called out to him as the car pulled away.

Karl had grown up in the small farming village. His parents knew he was slow, but they did not treat him differently from their other children. He went to the village school with his brothers and sisters. The teachers at the school knew that Karl was slower than the other children, but he was well-behaved and eager to learn. They did not fuss over his inability to learn as quickly as others. When he came home from school he helped his father on the farm along with his brothers and sisters. He made friends easily. No one singled him out or made him feel that he could not do the things that other youngsters could.

When the Nazis took over the school system, young people like Karl were no longer allowed to go to school. His father did not protest; he did not want to draw attention to Karl and his difficulties. He told Karl he needed him to do more work on the farm.

Karl was not unhappy; in fact, he preferred working on the farm to going to school. He kept the barn clean, fed and milked the cows and delivered butter, milk and eggs to the neighbors. Sometimes his sister gave him lessons so he would not forget how to read and write. Karl was happy with his life.

It was a long ride to the old gray stone building that was the state institution, a hospital and home for children and young people with disabilities. As soon as Karl stepped inside the hospital, a nurse took away his suitcase and shaved his head. She gave him a gray and white shirt and gray trousers and ordered him to change his clothes. The nurses and attendants seemed cold and indifferent. No one called him by his name. Karl felt lost. The woman who was the supervising nurse took Karl to a long narrow room with a row of fifteen beds on each side. She showed Karl the bed that was assigned to him and told him to join the line of boys waiting in the hallway outside the room. It was time for dinner and the boys were being marched to the dining hall.

The dining hall was a large room filled with wooden

tables. Ten boys sat at each table and ate their food in silence. No talking was allowed. Karl looked around him. All the boys had shaved heads and wore the same uniforms. Some were very young; others were older, like Karl. He asked the boy sitting next to him his name. Before the boy could answer, a supervisor came over to the table and scolded, "No talking allowed. Just eat your food." The boys had to eat quickly, because another group was waiting their turn for dinner.

To Karl, who had never been away from his family, who had never eaten a meal without laughter and chatter, the institution felt like a jail. Right after dinner, the boys were sent to bed. Karl could hear the boy in the bed next to him sobbing. He struggled to suppress his own panic and to ignore the fear that welled up inside of him. He comforted himself with thoughts about his family and life on the farm. He told himself that if he did as he was told, he would be allowed to go home again.

Every day more young people were brought to the state hospital and the wards were crowded with children of all ages. Some slept on straw mats on the floor. The food was drab and tasteless and there was never enough to eat. All the boys who were not in wheelchairs or bedridden were given jobs to do. They swept and scrubbed floors, collected garbage, washed dishes and did laundry. There was little to do in the institution but work, and everyone worked from early in the morning until lunch. Then they worked again until it was time for dinner. There were no games or other recreational activities. Sometimes in the evening they marched around the grounds singing Nazi songs and raising their arms in a Hitler salute. Karl kept to himself until he met Peter.

Karl met the tall friendly boy when he was assigned

to garbage collection. While most of the boys were given different work assignments each day, Peter had a regular job as an assistant to the janitor. He was the first person who called Karl by name and took an interest in him. Kind and patient, he was always willing to help when the bags of garbage were too big or heavy for Karl. Whenever they worked together, Peter made Karl laugh by making funny faces and telling him stories. The janitor let Peter pick his own helper, and he chose Karl.

Life was still rough, but Peter gave him confidence. Karl had a friend.

After they had worked together for a few months, Peter went to have an operation. When he came back he was given permission to go home. Karl knew that the operation was to make it impossible for Peter ever to become a father. Some of the older boys who had had the operation were allowed to leave the hospital and return to their families. Once back home, most of them were assigned menial jobs, sweeping and cleaning the streets, or collecting garbage in the towns and cities.

The day Peter left he gave Karl a paper with his name and address written neatly on it. He told Karl if he were ever able to leave the institution, to come and see him. Peter lived in the neighboring village only a few miles away.

Karl carefully folded the paper and put it in his pocket. At night he tucked the paper under his pillow, and every morning he put it back in his pocket. He missed Peter and tried to be like him and make life easier for the boys who worked with him. He helped the smaller boys and told them the funny stories Peter had told him.

When he had time, he visited with the children in

wheelchairs. When he went to collect the big bags of refuse from the dormitories, he stopped to talk to those who lay in their beds. Some could not talk, but Karl tried to get them to smile. Those who could not walk were kept in bed all day long with nothing to do. If he paused by a bed too long, the nurse on duty yelled at him, "Mind your own business and just take care of the garbage." But Karl always managed to wink or smile at the children as he carried out the heavy sacks. He knew how lucky he was that he did not have to depend on the nurses to eat or get dressed.

Karl worked from morning to evening. Without Peter, the work was boring and tedious. There was so much garbage to be picked up from all the crowded dormitories and brought to the big garbage bin behind the building. After lunch, garbage had to be collected from the kitchen, and then the floors of the kitchen and dining hall had to be swept and scrubbed.

A new janitor replaced the man who had worked with Peter. He was a big, fat fellow who bullied everyone and called the boys "idiots" and "morons." He pushed, slapped and punched the boys when they did not work quickly enough to suit him. Everyone had to do the dirty work while the janitor sat and drank from a bottle he kept in his pocket. Karl worked as fast as he could and tried to stay out of the man's way.

One afternoon as Karl was carrying a sack of garbage to the bin, he saw the janitor beating a boy with a broomstick. "I will teach you not to make a dirty mess," he shouted, punching the boy hard. Without thinking, Karl hurled the bag of garbage he was holding, hitting the janitor in the head and knocking him down. The garbage spilled over him.

Knowing he would be punished, Karl ran around to the other side of the building and hid in a barrel. Barely able to breathe, he sat hunched in the bottom. He froze when he heard footsteps and shouting and cursing. But then it was quiet. He stayed in the barrel a long time before he climbed out.

It was late in the afternoon; no one was outside. He knew he would be punished if he went back into the building. The janitor would beat him. He knew he had to escape. Karl ran down the path that led to the road. He did not stop running until he was away from the institution. He did not know where he was or where he was going. Then he remembered the paper in his pocket. It was getting dark and he could barely see to read the name of the village. He began running again. Peter had told him his home was in the next village. Despite the dark and the chill in the air, Karl did not stop to rest until he came to a sign that had the name of Peter's village on it.

He came to a row of houses. Peter had said he lived in a brown house, but Karl couldn't make out the colors of the houses in the dark. He passed a street with a few shops and saw a man sweeping the street in front of his store. Taking a deep breath, Karl approached and showed him the paper. The man pointed to a narrow lane. "It's the third house," he said.

Karl ran to the house, knocked loudly on the door and called Peter's name. A woman's voice called out, "Who is there?"

Karl waited at the door, hoping Peter would open it. Instead, a woman opened the door and stared at the disheveled, breathless boy who was beginning to tremble.

"Please, I want Peter, I look for Peter," Karl was almost

sobbing as he showed the woman the paper. By his clothing, the woman knew that the frightened boy must have run away from the institution. She pulled Karl inside and quickly closed the door.

"Peter told me to come to see him. Please tell him I am here. I am Karl."

Peter stepped into the room and Karl rushed to him. "It's me—Karl. You remember me, you gave me the paper and told me to come to you."

"Did you run away?" Peter asked, and put his arm around Karl.

"They going to punish me bad. The janitor beat the boy and I threw garbage at him. So I run away fast," Karl explained, his words tumbling out.

Peter nodded. "You did a good thing, Karl. You did right. I'm glad you are here."

Peter's mother took Karl to the kitchen and gave him a glass of warm milk and some bread and cheese.

"You can stay here tonight," she said, and watched him stuff the bread into his mouth. She made a bed for Karl on the sofa. Feeling safe and secure, he fell into a deep sleep.

Early the next morning, Peter woke Karl and gave him a clean shirt, trousers and a sweater.

"My brother, Hans, will take care of you. I'll be able to visit you at my brother's place too," he told him. Peter worked as a garbage collector in the village and had to leave before the sun was up.

Karl got up and dressed. Peter's mother gave him a plate of eggs and toast. While he was eating, she explained that Peter's older brother was coming to take him to a place where he would be safe.

"I want to go home," Karl said. "Please help me go to

my family." Peter's mother explained that the police would be looking for him in his home village.

"It is safer for you and your family if you live for a while where no one knows you," she said. "Hans will take good care of you. Please do not worry," she added.

Almost as soon as he had finished eating, a tall, handsome man who looked a lot like Peter came into the house.

Hans shook Karl's hand. He knew that his brother's friend had run away from the institution. "Have you ever worked on a farm?" he asked.

Karl nodded. "I like to work on a farm. I work on my father's farm."

"Then you can help my friend," Hans replied. Karl climbed into the back of the truck and Hans covered him with a pile of hay. "No one will find you now," he reassured him.

Karl lay on the floor and felt each bump on the long ride, but he felt safe with Peter's brother. When they reached the farm, Hans helped Karl climb down from the truck and took him to a small farmhouse. He introduced him to a farmer and his wife. "These people are good friends, but they cannot pay you. They'll let you stay with them until we can get you an identification paper." Every German boy over the age of sixteen years had to have an identification card in order to work. Karl did not have one and did not know how to get one.

"You show me that you can do good work and I'll get you work on other farms too. Then you can earn some money," the farmer told him.

Karl was eager to show the farmer how capable he was. He cleaned the barn, spread new hay on the barn floor, fixed a broken fence and cleaned the shed where the farmer kept his tools. That night he slept in the cellar of the farmer's house. It was cold, but Karl wrapped himself in a blanket. He felt safe.

The next morning he got up early. He washed his face and hands in a bucket of water and went upstairs for breakfast. He was surprised to see Hans in the kitchen.

"My friend tells me you do good work," he said. "But we need to get you an identification paper. Some of the farmers around here will get suspicious if they know you don't have a paper. If they think you escaped from somewhere, they will report you." Hans told him that the priest in the village would be willing to help, but first he wanted to meet Karl. Hans drove him to a small church where the priest was waiting for them.

"Why don't you have an identification paper?" the priest asked him.

"I did not know I need a paper," Karl explained.

"Everyone is given an identification paper," the priest said. "If you want me to help, you must tell me the truth."

Karl put his hands on his face and cried out, "I run away from bad place. They hit people there and I not go back. I want to go home."

The priest had heard about the terrible conditions in the institution from the nuns who were sometimes allowed to visit there. He told Karl he would try to get him a paper.

"If I have a paper, could I go back to my home?" Karl asked. "I know my parents want me to be home."

"If the police are looking for you, your family would be in great danger if you went home. It would be too easy to find you," the priest said quietly. "You'll need to stay on the farm for a while."

Karl nodded. He did not want to be caught and he did not want to put his family in danger.

The next day the priest brought Karl an identification paper. Karl looked at the neatly typed paper and did not recognize the name that was printed on it. The priest explained that Karl had a new name now and that he must remember it. With his identification paper, Karl was able to find more work on the neighboring farms and make some money.

When the first snows came and there was no more work on the farms, the priest found him a job in a nearby market and let him sleep in the church. He managed to contact Karl's family and tell them that their son was safe.

Karl carried his identification paper with him and did not forget his new name.

When the war was over, Karl was reunited with his family. There was a big party in the village to celebrate his return. He worked on the farm with his father and married a girl in the village.

* * *

The Nazi government removed thousands of children and adults from their homes in Germany. People with mental or physical disabilities were considered to be "unworthy of life." They were forced to work in large state hospitals and institutions, and many thousands were put to death.

12 Maria

GREECE

Finding independence
as a Greek Resistance Fighter

Maria stood with her classmates at the edge of the crowd. People were coming from all directions to Constitution Square in the center of Athens. Looking around, Maria saw men in suits and men in overalls, women with children, old people and young people standing together. They were protesting against the German occupation of Athens.

Athens had been occupied by the Germans since 1942. The Nazi flag now waved from the top of the Acropolis, the home of the Parthenon, the symbol of the ancient glory of Greece. The German army took its food supplies from the farms, leaving very little food for the people of Athens. People were hungry and came to protest.

A tall man in overalls took a bullhorn and spoke to the crowd. "We are faced with starvation and slavery and we must fight with all our hearts and our strength, for life and for freedom, so that our people might have bread," he shouted to the cheering crowd. "We will never be beaten," he said. "The Wingless Victory stands in front of the Parthenon to remind us that victory will never fly away from Athens." The statue stood before the Parthenon, an ancient marble temple built on top of the Acropolis.

Before the speaker could finish, German soldiers marched into the square. Pushing through the crowd, they fired their rifles into the air. People ran in all directions. Maria ran with her friends. On a street near the school, she saw a man being beaten by a German soldier. A younger man stepped out from behind a building and pushed the soldier away. Maria recognized him. He was a friend of her brothers, Stefanos and Manolis.

Maria's two older brothers were members of the *Andartes*, a group of Greek resistance fighters. They joined the Resistance as soon as they came home from the army. The Greek army defeated the Italian army in Albania and kept them from crossing the border into Greece. Everyone celebrated the victory with public parades and parties in the streets. A few weeks later, Germany invaded Greece.

An active resistance movement was quickly organized in Greece. "Nowhere else in Europe do people support their resistance fighters like the Greeks," her father had told her proudly when her brothers joined the *Andartes*.

"I wish I could be a resistance fighter too," Maria told her father.

"Girls are not supposed to fight. They have their own work to do," he said, and smiled at her.

Maria shook her long black hair and looked at her

father. "Papa, you know that Athens is named after a woman, the goddess Athena," she reminded him. "She is the symbol of wisdom and intelligence."

"Athena looked to her father Zeus for his wisdom. She carried out her father's wishes," her father insisted.

"She invented the flute and the plow, hurled thunderbolts and protected warriors," Maria replied.

"You are too serious for a young girl. You are not yet sixteen but you fill your pretty head with things that shouldn't concern you," he said, and picked up his newspaper.

"You have old-fashioned ideas about women. I have something I want to tell you," Maria said, softening her voice.

"What is it now?" he said with a sigh.

"Papa, I want to study at the university. I'm going to take the senior high school entrance examination to attend the *Lykea*. If I do well in my studies, will you let me go to the university?"

"I do not stop you from going to the *Gymnasio*, but I refuse to treat you like a boy," her father said sternly. "The country is in turmoil. Your brothers are living in a forest. Let us have peace and let them come home safely. Now go and help your mother," he said, dismissing her.

Papa doesn't know how determined I am, she thought to herself. Very few Greek girls went to the *Lykea*. Most girls finished their schooling after graduating from the *Gymnasio*. Maria's father was a lawyer and could afford to pay the tuition for the senior high school. Girls from poor families left school even before they finished their studies at the junior high school.

Maria took the examination for the *Lykea* with three

other girls. She passed the exam with high marks. She could go to the senior high school and prepare for university studies. If only Papa will be happy for me, she thought as she hurried home. She lived in a lovely old section of the city, where the gracious homes were covered with bougainvillea.

As Maria opened the door, she smelled the sweet spicy aroma of her mother's cooking. She put her books down and rushed into the kitchen. Her mother and grandmother were busy slicing tomatoes and onions. "I've been admitted to the *Lykea*," she told them. "If I do well, I'll be able to go to university."

"Oh, Maria, I'm happy for you," her mother said. Her grandmother jumped up, wiped her hands on her apron and hugged Maria.

"*Poulaka mou,* my little bird. I am so proud of you. You'll be the first girl in our family to go to the *Lykea*. You have given us something to celebrate tonight."

"Will Papa let me go? He doesn't think it is important for girls to go to school," Maria asked her mother.

"Your father won't stop you. He won't dare," her grandmother said, laughing.

"I still have a little influence on your father," her mother added, and showed her a tray of dolmathes, grape leaves stuffed with rice and meat.

"Where did you get all this food? It's been so long since we ate dolmathes. Just looking at them makes me hungry," Maria said happily. Her grandmother lived next door to a shopkeeper who put aside extra vegetables for his family and neighbors.

"I just hope they'll taste like real dolmathes. I had so little meat. Your grandmother brought me tomatoes, onions and fresh cheese," her mother answered. Maria saw her mother's expression change. She stopped smiling and said sadly, "If only your brothers could be home with us. I pray they are safe."

"Let's be happy tonight. Maria has given us something to celebrate," her grandmother said in a cheerful voice.

Maria's father came home with her uncle and everyone sat down at the long dining table. Her mother brought the green salad with fresh cheese, a plate of baked macaroni and the dolmathes to the table.

"We are going to have a good meal tonight," her father said with a grin. "It looks like we're having a celebration."

"We are celebrating. Maria has been accepted into the *Lykea*," her grandmother said proudly.

Maria's father looked at his daughter. "I am proud that you did so well in school, but I pray that you do not forget you are a young woman who will someday be a loving wife and mother," he said.

Maria felt her cheeks grow hot and knew she was blushing. "Will you let me go to the *Lykea*, Papa?" she asked.

Her father smiled, "Of course, I'll let you go, but I make no promises about the university," he said. Maria thanked him, then went to help her mother and grandmother wash and dry the dishes and pots.

Her father and uncle went into the parlor. Maria heard them talking.

"The Nazis are going to send Greek men and boys to work in German factories," her father said.

"Every day the Nazis think of something else to make us suffer," replied her uncle. He was a supervisor at a factory where the workers had held a protest rally. Maria overheard her uncle say that the men who had organized the rally had been arrested.

"If they'd let women join the Resistance, the war would be over faster," Maria whispered to her grandmother.

"Our Greek traditions are not easy to change." Her grandmother told her that when she was growing up, her neighbors had made fun of her father for letting her go to school. Maria's grandmother had been a nurse and had to stop working when she married her grandfather.

"In ancient Greece there were women warriors. We don't even know our own traditions. It's wrong to keep girls like prisoners in their own homes," Maria said, as she put the dishes away in the cupboard.

At school, there was talk about forming a girls' group to help the resistance fighters. Maria's teacher told the girls about the "Free Young Women," the *Eleftheri Nea* (EN) that was being organized at the school. Maria went to the first meeting with her friends.

"Girls, Greece needs you," the teacher announced. "We are organizing soup kitchens for children in the poorer districts of Athens."

Maria wanted to sign up with her friends. Diana was sixteen and did not need permission. The teacher gave Maria a permission form. She folded it neatly and tucked it into her school bag. She knew it would not be easy to get her father to sign it for her.

She decided to wait until after dinner to show her father the form. After dinner, she went into the parlor, where her father was reading a book.

"Papa, I have something very important to show you," she said, holding out the paper. Her father sighed and put his book down.

"What can be so important?" he asked.

"I need your permission to join a girls' club," she explained. "We'll be doing good work. We're going to organize a soup kitchen and feed hungry children. Most of my friends have signed up already." Maria gave him the permission slip.

"Please let me join. You know yourself how many people are dying from hunger."

Her father read the form. "I don't know," he said. "This sounds as if it could be dangerous. You should not be out of the school or the house on your own. Young girls should be accompanied by their fathers or brothers."

"Papa, you said you were proud of me for being a good student. Now let me make you proud by doing something to help other people," Maria said, and gave her father a pen.

"You can be so stubborn—you won't let me have any peace until I sign," he said. "You must promise me that you will be very careful."

"Oh, I will, Papa," she said happily, and took the form.

With her father's signature, Maria was accepted into the EN. She went to a training session with Diana. The teacher explained how the soup kitchens were to be organized.

"Everyone in the community wants to help. Local storekeepers are donating the food. We will bring it to the schools and prepare it in the school kitchens," the teacher explained. The girls had a cooking lesson and learned to make potato soup, cereal and pancakes.

The next day, Maria and two other girls went to set up a soup kitchen in a school in the poorest district in

Athens. Close to the downtown area, the district was hidden behind the beautiful old university complex and the National Museum. To get there the girls had to walk past the central market. Maria noticed how empty the shops were.

"Our families cannot buy all the food they want, but here people have no food at all," Maria said, noticing the squalor of the district. The houses were crowded together on narrow, crooked streets. Windows were broken and garbage littered the alleyways. The old school building looked broken down too.

The teachers in the school greeted them and showed them where to set up. The small kitchen in the back of the school building had an old stove where the girls prepared the food. They improvised a dining room in the school gymnasium with old tables and chairs. The first day, twenty children crowded into the room. When they were seated the girls served them each a bowl of soup and a slice of bread.

"These children are so hungry. They can't eat fast enough," Maria whispered to another girl as they watched the children empty their bowls and gobble up the bread. Every day more children came to the soup kitchen.

Housewives from the neighborhood came to help and brought what little food they could spare. Storekeepers supplied them with potatoes and onions and the girls collected greens and mixed them with cornmeal to make pancakes for the children.

"Everyone wants to help," Maria told her mother, who gave her flour and chickpeas to take to the school. The soup kitchen was a big success.

More and more girls joined the EN. Some of them

were students in high school; others worked in the factories or stayed at home. During the summer, the EN merged with a larger group called the *Enaia Panelladhiki Organosi Neon* (EPON), the United Panhellenic Organization of Youth. Maria continued to work in the soup kitchen and tutored girls who did not know how to read or write. Maria and Diana went to other neighborhoods in Athens and made announcements on street corners to recruit girls to work in the soup kitchens.

In the fall, Maria began her studies at the senior high school. She was now a member of the student group of EPON. Not only did they help in the soup kitchens, but they also organized protest rallies and wrote slogans on the streets. Diana was a member of the same student group.

The girls would go out in groups of four to write slogans. Two girls did the writing and the other two stood guard. If they saw a German soldier, the girls standing guard would hum a tune. It was a signal to stop and hide. They knew the people who lived in the neighborhood would not give them away.

Going to protest rallies and recruiting other girls to help in the soup kitchens kept Maria very busy. She often had to stay up late at night to complete her school work.

"Did you know that some of the girls in EPON are bringing weapons to resistance camps in the hills close to Athens? They stuff the weapons in their school bags and hike up the mountainside." Diana told her about a street battle that had taken place in Kaissarani, a suburb of Athens. Many members of EPON were arrested and sent to jail along with other captured resistance fighters.

At an EPON meeting the girls were told that a few prisoners who understood German were getting important information from the guards. "We'll take food to the prisoners and carry messages out of the prison. We'll learn more about what the Germans are planning," the EPON leader told them.

Maria volunteered to deliver food to the prisoners. The first time she went to the jail she was tense and frightened. She had never been to a prison before. The jail was in an old brick building with a guard posted at the iron gate. Maria tried to appear calm as she answered his questions and let him inspect the bag of food she was carrying. He gave her permission to go into the prison.

The air in the old prison building was musty. Men sat in small jail cells. She went from cell to cell handing out small parcels of food. Maria was on the lookout for any prisoner who had a message. A young man with curly black hair motioned to her to come close and whispered, "Tell my brother to hide; the Gestapo are planning to raid the factory where he works." Maria nodded to indicate she would deliver the message, and moved to the next cell. As soon as she left the jail, she took the message straight to the EPON leader. Every week she carried food to the jail, sometimes alone, sometimes with another girl.

"Being in EPON has given me wings," she told her father. "Now I understand what justice really means. I feel like a real woman now, not just a girl."

"Please be careful. German soldiers kill girls as easily as boys," her father warned, but he did not stop her.

Maria felt closer to her father. His attitude was changing and he showed her more respect. When she was made a leader of the EPON group, her father told her he was proud of her.

Without carrying weapons or making a big fuss, the girls in the Resistance were on the front lines. They took wounded people to the hospitals, operated soup kitchens, led protest marches and fed the resistance fighters. They developed their own resources and made their own plans.

Maria worked for the Resistance until the end of the war.

After the war, Maria graduated from the *Lykea* and went to university. Her brothers came home and the family was together again. She never forgot her experiences in EPON. She thought that they had liberated her as much as they had helped her country.

References

Burleigh, Michael. *Death And Deliverance: Euthanasia in Germany 1900-1945*. Cambridge: Cambridge UP, 1994.

Ehrlich, Blake. *Resistance France, 1940-1945*. Boston: Little, Brown, 1965.

Fonseca, Isabel. *Bury Me Standing: The Gypsies and Their Journey*. New York: Vintage Books, 1996.

Goldberger, Leo, ed. *The Rescue of the Danish Jews: Moral Courage Under Stress*. New York: New York University Press, 1987.

Goetz, A., P. Chroust and C. Pross, eds. *Cleansing the Fatherland: Nazi Medicine and Racial Hygiene*. Baltimore: Johns Hopkins UP, 1994.

Harrington, Lyn. *Greece and the Greeks*. New York: Thomas Nelson, 1962.

Hart, Janet. *New Voices in the Nation: Women and the Greek Resistance, 1941-1964*. Ithaca, NY: Cornell UP, 1996.

Holmes, Blair R. and Alan F. Keele, eds. *When Truth was Treason: German Youth Against Hitler, The Story of the Helmuth Huebener Group*. Urbana and Chicago: University of Illinois Press, 1995.

Kaplan, Marion A. *Between Dignity and Despair: Jewish Life in Nazi Germany.* New York: Oxford UP, 1998.

Levine, Ellen. *Darkness Over Denmark: The Danish Resistance and the Rescue of Jews.* New York: Holiday House, 2000.

Ligeois, Jean Pierre. *Gypsies: An Illustrated History.* London: Al Saqi Books, 1986.

Lusseyran, Jacques. *And Then There Was Light.* New York: Little, Brown, 1965.

Perrault, Gille and Pierre Azema. *Paris Under Occupation.* New York: The Vendome Press, 1989.

Peukert, D.J.K. *Inside Nazi Germany: Conformity, Opposition and Social Life in the Third Reich.* London: Batsford, 1987.

Read, Anthony and David Fisher. *The Fall of Berlin.* New York: Norton, 1992.

Rogow, Sally M. "Child Victims in Nazi Germany," *Journal of Holocaust Education.* Vol. 8 No. 3 (Winter 1999), pp. 71-86.

Shiber, Etta with Anne and Paul Dupré. *Paris Underground.* New York: Charles Scribner and Sons, 1943.

Tomasevic, Neboojsa Bato and Raijko Djuric. *Gypsies of the World: A Journey into the Hidden World of Gypsy Life and Culture.* New York: Henry Holt, 1988.

Yoors, Jan. *Crossing.* New York: Simon and Shuster, 1971; Prospect Heights, Illinois: Waveland, 1988.

Glossary

Allies Countries fighting against Nazi Germany

The Andartes A group of Greek resistance fighters *(MARIA)*

Arbeitskarte German work permit *(JACOB)*

Athena Goddess of Greek mythology *(MARIA)*

Auschwitz Notorious Nazi death camp located inside Poland *(JACOB)*

BBC British Broadcasting Corporation issuing news of the war *(HELMUT HUEBENER)*

Buchenwald Nazi concentration and extermination camp in Germany *(JACQUES LUSSEYRAN)*

de Gaulle, Charles Leader of the Free French Forces during WWII, later president of France *(JACQUES LUSSEYRAN)*

EN – Eleftheri Nea The "Free Young Women" resistance movement in Greece *(MARIA)*

EPON – Enaia Panelladhiki Organosi Neon The United Pan-Hellenic Organization of Youth that merged with the EN in Greece *(MARIA)*

Fresnes Prison A French prison used by the Nazis *(JACQUES LUSSEYRAN)*

German Maidens Nazi organization for girls *(ANNELIESE)*

Gestapo The secret police of Nazi Germany *(LOUISE)*

Gymnasio Greek schools for grades six through nine *(MARIA)*

Hadamar Psychiatric hospital in northern Germany; one of six Nazi killing sites of people with mental illness and physical handicaps *(NONI)*

Jungvolk Nazi youth groups for boys under fourteen years of age *(EDELWEISS PIRATES)*

Lykea Senior high schools in Greece *(MARIA)*

Majdanek Notorious death camp in Poland *(JACOB)*

Nazi Youth German boys between fourteen and eighteen were required to join *(EDELWEISS PIRATES)*

Ploetzonsee Infamous German prison where inmates were executed *(HELMUT HUEBENER)*

Pyrénées Mountains Mountain range separating France and Spain *(YOJO)*

Rom or Roma and Sinti Proper names for Gypsies *(YOJO)*

SS *(Schutzstaffel)* A military unit of the Nazi Party; the SS were security police and concentration camp guards *(JACOB)*

Treblinka Nazi death camp in Poland *(JACOB)*

U-Boat Name used to describe Jewish youth in hiding in Germany *(LOUISE)*

Wehrmacht German military *(JACOB)*

Yad Vashem Israeli Holocaust Memorial and Documentation Center *(JACOB)*

Zeus Powerful god of Greek mythology *(MARIA)*

About the author

Sally Rogow has a keen interest in stories of heroism. Her experience working with children with disabilities gave her many opportunities to witness the courage of young people facing adversity. Educator and author, Sally Rogow has written books and articles on language development, literacy, play and social development as well as stories and books for children and young people. *Lillian Wald: The Nurse In Blue* and *Rosa Minoka Hill, Native Woman Physician* are two of her titles.

Sally Rogow has a B.A. from the University of Wisconsin, an M.A. from Columbia University, an M.A. from Michigan State and an Ed.D. from the University of British Columbia. A native New Yorker, she now lives in Vancouver, B.C.